PELICAN BOOKS

AID AS IMPERIALISM

Teresa Hayter was born in 1940 in Shanghai. She went with
her parents to Washington, London, Paris and Moscow.
She received a conventionally upper middle class education,
including three wasted years at Oxford University, where,
thanks, as her tutor said, to 'luck and native wit', she got a
'second' in so-called Modern History. Her education began
with travel: round the world in sixteen months in search
of insecurity, in pre-hippy travel days, which made clear the
existence of cultures and values other than those of the
British bourgeoisie. She was steadily employed from 1963
to 1968 by the Overseas Development Institute, which com-
missioned her to write books on French Aid and the World
Bank in Latin America, published the former but not the
latter (see Appendix), and sent her to West Africa, Latin
America and Paris. She was then less steadily employed by
Nuffield College, which sent her to Kenya and financed an
abortive attempt to do a post-graduate course in bourgeois
economics. She is now a member of the International Marxist
Group and is on the editorial board of the *Red Mole*.

AID AS IMPERIALISM

TERESA HAYTER

PENGUIN BOOKS

Penguin Books Ltd, Harmondsworth, Middlesex, England
Penguin Books Inc., 7110 Ambassador Road, Baltimore, Maryland 21207 U.S.A.
Penguin Books Australia Ltd, Ringwood, Victoria, Australia

—

First published 1971
Reprinted 1972, 1974

—

Copyright © Teresa Hayter, 1971

—

Made and printed in Great Britain
by C. Nicholls & Company Ltd
Set in Monotype Times

CONTENTS

FOREWORD

THERE is a dying belief that aid is a form of disinterested international munificence. Those who cling to this view fly in the face of clear evidence of its role as a weapon of the foreign policy of the 'donor' countries. Remarkably little attempt is made to disguise this fact. For instance, President Kennedy said in 1961 that 'foreign aid is a method by which the United States maintains a position of influence and control around the world, and sustains a good many countries which would definitely collapse, or pass into the Communist bloc'. And a former senior economist of the US Agency for International Development, Professor H. B. Chenery, has admitted that 'economic assistance is one of the instruments of foreign policy that is used to prevent political and economic conditions from deteriorating in countries where we value the preservation of the present government'.

Such motivations explain why more American aid has gone to South Vietnam than to any other country. This is not an exceptional case; it simply reveals in an exceptionally ugly way the purposes to which aid may be put; the difference between this and other cases is merely that in Vietnam a nation is resisting these purposes.

Many people, disillusioned by these facts, now have great hopes for the redirection of aid through international agencies such as the World Bank; aid would thus, it is hoped, lose its association with the foreign policy of nations.

The holders of such hopes are in for a nasty shock when they read this book. The World Bank is growing rapidly, fed largely by funds from Western capital markets. Most of its loans are at commercial rates of interest. In the next five years it will certainly 'give' more 'aid' than the US government. And full repayment of its loans is essential to the Bank's continued existence. It has, therefore, a vested interest against socialist or nationalist policies which might lead to nationalization and default. In Latin America in particular the obligations of governments to repay and service old

5

loans, and the demands of capitalist corporations to repatriate their profits, are overtaking the capacity of these economies to earn foreign exchange. This makes nationalization and default a growing temptation to any country not dominated by imperialism.

The Bank's very existence requires the prevention of default, which is, in an emergency, not within its physical power to enforce. It is, however, within the power of the United States and other Western governments. The policy of the Bank, therefore, is inevitably for this reason, among others, an integral part of the foreign policies of Western capitalist nations towards underdeveloped countries. One would, therefore, expect its powers of 'leverage' to be used in a way that is favourable to capitalism and free trade and against socialism and economic nationalism.

At present, as Teresa Hayter shows, it can be most clearly seen to be doing this in Latin-American countries.

These propositions cannot be proved by reference to figures in annual reports or to national accounts. To admit the validity of only that kind of evidence, as many economists do, is to contribute to the distortion of reality. Documentation in this case requires searching and sensitive inquiry, supported by a sophisticated analysis of the political mechanisms at work.

This is what Teresa Hayter has achieved in this interesting study – now available after an unfortunate delay, following the refusal of the Overseas Development Institute to publish it. The delay cannot have been due to the quality of the work. A draft was read carefully and very favourably reported on either to Teresa Hayter or to the ODI by at least five economists with some experience of work on the Third World. They all felt that it made a valuable and penetrating contribution to our knowledge of the activities in Latin America of international financial institutions which claim for themselves a major role in the fight against world poverty.

The World Bank has been happy to publicize the friendly reservations about international aid made by the Pearson Commission. By contrast, it has tried very hard to suppress Teresa Hayter's study. Fortunately it has failed; the strength of the attempt may be taken to indicate the accuracy of the analysis.

Oxford, 1970   R. B. SUTCLIFFE

PREFACE

THIS study was written while I was a member of the staff of the Overseas Development Institute (ODI), and was intended for publication by them. It was financed mainly by the World Bank, which paid my salary at the ODI and my expenses in Latin America and Washington. With the exception of some minor editorial changes, especially in the last section of Chapter 4, and the addition of an Appendix, it is published here in the form in which it was submitted to, and finally rejected by, the ODI.[1]

Research at the ODI was based on the assumption that 'aid' was good and that the major objective of 'aid' could reasonably be expected to be 'development' in, and for, the Third World. Aid could be criticized for falling short of this objective, and proposals could be made for improving its contribution to development. But the central assumption was that the imperialist countries were 'helping' the Third World to develop. The possibility that they were, on the contrary, stunting and distorting development in the Third World through exploitation, and that the Third World could not develop until imperialism was destroyed, was not considered. Nor could it be, since ODI, like aid, is merely the smooth face of imperialism.

The ODI claims to be 'an independent non-government body aiming to ensure wise action in the field of overseas development'. It is financed by the Ford Foundation, by British companies with interests in the Third World, and,

1. Under the title: *Leverage: The World Bank, the International Monetary Fund and the United States Agency for International Development in Latin America.*

7

intermittently, by institutions such as the Nuffield Foundation, the Rockefeller Foundation and the World Bank. Its Council consists largely of representatives of the British companies providing money, together with representatives of the, more or less, liberal establishment. The former have a direct financial interest in increases in the size of aid. The latter, presumably, have some sort of philanthropic interest in aid, with or without an interest in international order and stability, and, in general, in the continued existence of capitalism. Probably no member of the Council would be prepared to contemplate the collapse of capitalism, and most are strongly committed to its preservation. Hence their support for aid. The research staff of the ODI were mainly liberals concerned to promote increased welfare in the Third World, and thoroughly misled and mystified as to the means of achieving it. Such was I.

It was possible for the staff of the ODI to work for the ODI authorities with a fair degree of harmony and satisfaction so long as they failed to understand that welfare in the Third World was not compatible with the continued existence of imperialist exploitation. I had written a book on French aid which fell easily within the ODI's ideological framework; while giving a spurious impression of factual description, it obscured the real nature of the relationship of France with its semi-colonial dependencies in Africa. Similarly, in an account which I wrote of the proceedings of a conference, I reported with some sympathy the idea that aid should be used as a 'lever' to induce its recipients to adopt particular economic policies;[2] together with other members of ODI staff, I was prepared to regard this idea as 'progressive', a step forward in the world development effort.

Since being in Latin America I have come slowly to

2. See *Effective Aid*, ODI, 1966.

realize that such assumptions and values constitute a complicated edifice of deception: deception of the sort which
enables the capitalist classes throughout the world to
exploit the masses with a fine sense of the justice of their
position, and of the nobility of their purposes. A study of
aid ought to start from a more honest appraisal of reality.
I believe, now, that the existence of aid can be explained
only in terms of an attempt to preserve the capitalist system
in the Third World. Aid is not a particularly effective
instrument for achieving this; hence its current decline.
But, in so far as it is effective, its contribution to the well-
being of the peoples of the Third World is negative, since it
is not in their interest that exploitation should continue.
Any contributions to their well-being which may arise
through aid are incidental to its main purposes, and must
be balanced against its generally negative effect. Aid can be
regarded as a concession by the imperialist powers to
enable them to continue their exploitation of the semi-
colonial countries; it is similar in its effects to reforms
within capitalist countries, in the sense that the exploiting
classes relinquish the minimum necessary in order to
retain their essential interests. The availability of 'official
aid' increases the likelihood that the governments of Third
World countries will tolerate the continuation of massive
outflows of private profits and interest on past debts. It may
help to bolster up such governments by providing a few
short-term solutions to their economic difficulties. It may
also help to create and sustain, within Third World countries, a class which is dependent on the continued existence
of aid and foreign private investment and which therefore
becomes an ally of imperialism.

From the point of view of those receiving it, aid has a
number of additional disadvantages. For example, it can be
used directly as a bribe to secure the adoption of measures

favourable to the providers of aid and unfavourable to its recipients; it can be used, deliberately or otherwise, for projects which impoverish the mass of the population; and it usually adds to the burden of debt carried by the countries receiving it, and hence to their dependence. In one sense, aid is merely a form of subsidy for international companies paid for by the tax-payers of the imperialist countries. An obvious case is aid which is tied to exports from the country providing it, sometimes, as in the US case, specifically to those which are uncompetitive in world markets; goods which are financed by tied aid are usually very much more expensive than those which could be bought elsewhere. Aid also partially finances the profits and interest which are remitted in increasing amounts from the Third World. It may enlarge the overseas markets for the products of the private companies of the imperialist powers; and it can be used to secure the creation of facilities such as roads, harbours and training institutions, to commit the Third World's own resources to such projects, and thus to make the operations of these companies more profitable.

In its general role as preserver of the capitalist system, aid can act in more indirect and complex ways than as a mere bribe or concession to sweeten the pill of exploitation. It can be used in an attempt to build up social and economic systems considered to be durable and resistant to revolutionary change. At times its provision has been made conditional on certain reforms being adopted within Third World countries, particularly in the spheres of taxation, education, even land reform, which, it is hoped, will defuse potential revolutionary situations.[3] Aid can also be used in an attempt to secure, by attaching specific conditions, the smoother functioning of the system, and thus to ensure that debts are repaid, that profits can be remitted abroad and that

3. See quotations in Foreword.

restrictions on imports can be removed; it can also be used to avert disruptive crises.

This study is mainly concerned with attempts by the World Bank (or the International Bank for Reconstruction and Development, IBRD), the International Monetary Fund (IMF) and the United States Agency for International Development (AID) to use 'aid' in the last of these functions; it is also concerned with their failure to use it, as I had supposed that they might, to achieve reforms. The study is basically a liberal critique of aid policies. It developed into an attempt to expose the inconsistencies and conflicting motivations of these policies. But, at the time when I wrote it, I was far from de-mystified. The study suffers from the fact that I took official statements about aid at their face value, and criticized the international aid agencies for not doing what I had been naïve to expect them to do. It was written on the assumption that the well-being of the peoples of the Third World was, or at least could become, the primary consideration in aid policies. Since this assumption was invalid, much of the discussion of the errors and omissions of the international agencies, in chapter four for example, has a decidedly unrealistic air. The study was written with care and caution and a certain amount of evasion, since it had at least to give an appearance of being publishable by the ODI. It was also rewritten, at the behest of ODI, back to front, 'so as to present the agencies' case more fairly' (see Appendix).

The ODI was, nevertheless, unable to publish it. This was hardly surprising; it merely confirmed some of my theses about the real nature and purposes of aid and its supporting institutions, such as the ODI. That the ODI took so long to decide not to publish the study (see Appendix) perhaps also demonstrates the unreality of the world in which the directors and staff of the ODI live. The long history of the ODI's changes of mind and the World Bank's financial pressure, of which I have given an account in the Appendix, may be of interest only to those who are concerned about 'free speech' and who like small scandals around this issue. But it does provide some additional insight into the *modus operandi* of the World Bank, in particular, and in this sense it has some relevance to the study's contents. Given the mushrooming status of Mr McNamara's new instrument for preserving the 'Free World', all such insights have, I think, some interest.

LIST OF ABBREVIATIONS

AID	Agency for International Development
BID	Banco Interamericano de Desarrollo (or IADB)
CEPAL	Comisión Económica para America Latina (or ECLA)
CIA	Central Intelligence Agency
CIAP	Comité Interamericano de la Alianza para el Progreso (Inter-American Committee of the Alliance for Progress)
CIDA	Comité Interamericano de Desarrollo Agrícola
CORFO	Corporación de Fomento de la Producción (Chile)
ECLA	Economic Commission for Latin America (or CEPAL)
FAO	Food and Agriculture Organization
FRAP	Frente Acción Popular (Popular Action Front) (Chile)
IADB	Inter-American Development Bank (also BID or IDB)
IA–ECOSOC	Inter-American Economic and Social Council
IBRD	International Bank for Reconstruction and Development (World Bank)
IDA	International Development Association
IDB	Inter-American Development Bank (or IADB)
IFC	International Finance Corporation
IMF	International Monetary Fund
IPC	International Petroleum Company
OAS	Organisation of American States
OECD	Organisation for Economic Co-operation and Development
ODI	Overseas Development Institute
UNCTAD	United Nations Conference on Trade and Development

Chapter 1

CONCEPTS AND STATE OF THE DISCUSSION

'AID' has never been an unconditional transfer of financial resources. Usually the conditions attached to aid[1] are clearly and directly intended to serve the interests of the governments providing it. For example aid must generally be used to buy goods and services from its provider. Aid from the United States must be carried in United States ships. Aid from the United States is not, under the Hickenlooper Amendment, available to countries which nationalize US-owned assets and fail to 'take appropriate steps' to rectify the situation within six months.[2] Aid from the World Bank is not, under an internal Policy Memorandum which has not been published, available to countries which nationalize foreign-owned assets without compensation, which fail to repay their debts or in which there are claims on behalf of foreign investors which the Bank considers should be settled. Aid is, in general, available to countries whose internal political arrangements, foreign policy alignments, treatment of foreign private investment, debt-servicing record, export policies, and so on, are considered desirable, potentially desirable, or at least acceptable, by

1. The term 'aid' is currently used to describe transfers of resources from governments or official institutions to developing countries. It is used here, without inverted commas, because it is short, and in spite of its connotations.

2. 'Appropriate steps' can include 'speedy compensation' and 'arbitration'. See, for example, *Legislation on Foreign Relations, with Explanatory Notes*, printed for the use of the Committees on Foreign Relations and Foreign Affairs of the Senate and the House of Representatives, US Government Printing Office, Washington, 1965, p. 44.

the countries or institutions providing aid, and which do not appear to threaten their interests.

Some of the conditions attached to aid have also been justified in terms of the need to promote economic development in underdeveloped countries. Supporters of aid argue that promoting economic development in poor countries is in the long-term interests of the developed countries. Therefore they should try to ensure that development occurs.[3] The objective of development itself can be interpreted in different ways; some kinds of development in poorer countries are likely to benefit richer countries, or at least to be compatible with their interests; others are not, or so it is officially assumed. The subject of aid has been, and presumably will continue to be, peculiarly obfuscated by confusion about objectives. But even supposing an improvement in general standards of living were the only concern of the providers of aid, it could possibly still be argued that some effort should be made by developed

3. For example the *Program Guidance Manual* of the United States Agency for International Development (AID) states: 'Aid as an instrument of foreign policy is best adapted to promoting economic development. Development is not an end in itself, but it is a critical element in US policy, for in most countries some progress in economic welfare is essential to the maintenance and the growth of free, non-communist societies.' See also the UK White Paper, *Overseas Development: The Work of the New Ministry*, HMSO, August 1965, in which it is stated: 'But we must be clear about the political objectives which our aid programme can and cannot be expected to achieve. Aid is a means of promoting long-term economic development. ... Aid is not a means of winning the friendship of individual countries, though we are glad to offer aid to our friends ... Nevertheless, we must recognize that poverty in a world of growing wealth causes discontent and unrest to which economic and social development is the only possible answer. We must therefore be ready to share our wealth and knowledge so as to help promote the progress and strengthen the stability of the developing countries by increasing the material well-being of their peoples.'

countries to ensure that the resources they transferred did actually contribute to welfare in developing countries, and were not, for example, merely transferred to Swiss bank accounts, especially as aid competes with other claims on resources within industrialized countries.

This principle has sometimes been oddly applied. For example it has on occasion been used to justify the provision of aid in the form of loans rather than grants, on the grounds of the need to encourage financial discipline in developing countries.[4] Similarly with the practice of providing aid only for the direct foreign exchange costs of projects.[5] More credibly, the practice of tying aid to specific projects, whose choice and design must be negotiated and approved, has generally been regarded in developed countries as a means of ensuring a satisfactory use of resources, although it also, in the case of bilateral donors, provides a means of ensuring that aid promotes additional exports from themselves, and enables them to choose visible projects, on which their label can be displayed.

More recently, increasing importance has been attached to the idea that developed countries, or international institutions, should use their power to withhold or increase aid as a means of influencing the *general* economic policies of developing countries in specific directions. It is with this idea, and its application, that this study is concerned.

The argument is that to regard aid merely as a transfer of resources not only does not ensure that it is not wasted, but fails to make full use of the opportunities of promoting

4. The effectiveness of this discipline depends on the continued acknowledgement by developing countries of their obligation to repay their debts. On the debt burden in developing countries, see p. 173.

5. This practice tends to result in the choice of excessively import-intensive projects. See Juliet Clifford, 'The Tying of Aid and the Problem of "Local Costs"'. *Journal of Development Studies*, January 1966.

'satisfactory' economic policies that aid provides. Even insistence on choosing and financing particular projects, and perhaps on the adoption of other measures connected with the projects, will not adequately determine the use of the country's own resources. It will not prevent governments from financing other projects of which the donor may disapprove and in fact may enable them to do so, except in a few small countries with very low levels of savings; aid may thus, in practice, finance the marginal project.[6] Above all, the government's general economic policies probably have a much more significant effect than its choice of projects. Therefore aid, if used to influence these policies, can in theory act as a 'major catalyst' promoting development, or policies considered conducive to development or in other ways important. It is argued that donors, by attaching conditions to aid, should try to ensure that it does act in this way.

In so far as an attempt is made to use aid in this way, there are, broadly speaking, three possible alternatives. The agency administering aid can fail to agree with a government and decide that its policies are so unsatisfactory that it provides no aid, or stops or reduces existing aid.[7] It can agree with the government and merely provide aid to enable this government to carry out its policies, possibly suggesting modifications and improvements.[8] Or it can

6. Tying aid to projects, especially when only the direct foreign exchange cost of the project is financed, has other disadvantages, notably the possibility of making projects more capital- and import-intensive than they might otherwise be, and of distorting the pattern of imports so that existing capacity is not fully used.

7. The World Bank, the IMF and the US AID have, for example, reacted in this way in Cuba, in Brazil under Goulart, in Argentina under Illia, and in Haiti.

8. This was the case, for the World Bank, IMF and AID, in Brazil under President Castelo Branco and Dr Campos.

attempt to change the policies, usually in countries where it is considered that there are enough satisfactory elements for it to be worth supporting some policies against others and trying to 'improve' the government's total pro-gramme.[9] In the first two cases the decisions involved are mainly connected with the allocation of aid. In the last case, the aid agency or agencies attempt to work out their own solutions and policies for the country and to induce its government to adopt them. Of course the situations over-lap. An important feature of the decisions on aid allocation is the effect they are expected to have on the policies adopted by other governments hoping to receive aid; in fact it is, for the moment, as will be seen, reasonably clear which kind of economic policies are likely to be approved, political and other things being equal, and which are not. But increasing importance is attached to the more positive action involved in the third case, in actually changing a government's policies.

Those who support policies of this variety usually claim that the choice of economic policies is a reasonably tech-nical matter, on which sensible men can agree. They argue that it is possible for aid agencies, especially international agencies, to make objective decisions, free from political *arrière pensées*;[10] and that it is frequently easier for them to

9. This was, broadly, the case in Chile in the first years of the Frei government, and has been so in many other countries.

10. See Irving S. Friedman, in his introductory speech at a seminar held by four World Bank officials for Brazilian economists and re-produced in a World Bank publication, *Some Aspects of the Economic Philosophy of the World Bank*, September 1968: 'First, what strikes me as very important is that both institutions (the World Bank and the IMF) are set up with specific purposes and defined objectives, which make clear that if the institutions are to operate properly they must make economic judgements in specific fields of international responsi-bility and that these economic judgements are to be based on objective economic analysis. It is clear from the origins of both these institutions,

make such decisions and to press for them, than it is for national governments, which are distracted by internal political considerations. Their function is, according to this view, to provide the economic realism which otherwise might be lacking and to reinforce the position of those within the country who share this attribute.

It is sometimes also maintained that the promotion of 'better' economic policies can be achieved through discussion and 'dialogue' between governments and aid agencies, and through the close involvement of 'donors' in the choice of policies in the 'recipient' countries, but that the provision of aid should not be made conditional on the former agreeing with the latter.[11] But the idea of conditionality, or 'leverage' as it is called, is essential, and perhaps inherent, in the policies of the major financial agencies currently concerned with the general economic policies of developing countries. These are the World Bank, the International Monetary Fund (IMF), and the United States Agency for International Development (AID).[12]

These three institutions (which will be referred to as the

---

as well as the words of their Articles of Agreement, that they were not set up as political institutions. They were set up as technical institutions; and from the very first, great emphasis was given to the need for scientific, economic work as a basis for decision-making.' See also quotation p. 54.

11. See for example John White, *Pledged to Development*, ODI, 1967, especially pp. 180–86, in which it is suggested that the function of the providers of aid might be one of 'loyal opposition', whereby the donor 'does not seek to lay down the law' but to point out new issues and new choices. Also Andrzej Krassowski, *The Aid Relationship*, ODI, 1968, especially chapter 1, in which these themes are discussed and expanded, and the current practices of the United States AID are criticized on the grounds that they involve too great an attempt to 'control' recipients' policies.

12. The IMF is not usually regarded as an aid institution, and the rationale for its activities is rather different from those of the AID

'international agencies') are now deeply involved in the business of setting 'general performance' conditions on the use of their resources. They are widely respected in developed countries on the basis of very little knowledge of, and even less published material on, the agencies' views on development and their methods of inducing developing countries to adopt them. There is, in Latin America in particular, considerable public debate on the policies of the IMF, and the debate has made some impact on the Fund. But much less is known of the opinions and activities of the World Bank. In particular there is little awareness of the fact that both the World Bank and the AID are promoting policies in Latin America similar to those of the IMF. Moreover little has been published on the actual operations of the three institutions in this field.[13] The negotiations for

---

and the World Bank. But the activities themselves, in this field, are similar.

13. But see, for example, *Effective Aid*, ODI, 1966, *passim*; Andrzej Krassowski, op. cit., chapters 3–6; John White, op. cit., *passim*; *United States Foreign Aid in Action: A Case Study*, submitted by Senator Ernest Gruening to the Subcommittee on Foreign Aid Expenditures of the Committee on Government Operations, United States Senate, Washington, 1966, especially pp 102–14; various AID publications (see chapter 2, section on the AID); M. Hoffman, 'The Scaffolding of Aid', *Asian Review*, April 1968; David Gordon, 'The World Bank's Mission in Eastern Africa', *Finance and Development* (the Fund and Bank Review), No. 1, 1968; Richard Newton Gardner, *Sterling–Dollar Diplomacy*, Oxford, Clarendon Press, 1956; Raymond F. Mikesell, *Public International Lending for Development*, Random House, N.Y., 1966; Richard L. Maullin, 'The Colombia–IMF disagreement of November–December 1966: an interpretation of its place in Colombian politics', Memorandum RM–5314–RC, Rand Corporation, 1967; Marta Luisa Benavente, 'El Fondo Monetario Internacional, mecanismo de sus operaciones y posición de la República Argentina', *Revista Trimestral*, Banco Central de la República Argentina, July–September 1966; Neil H. Jacoby, *US Aid to Taiwan*, Praeger

the adoption of their policies are conducted in much secrecy, and the subject is a sensitive one.

Similarly, although there are possibly more inhibitions outside these agencies, it is nevertheless quite widely assumed in developed countries that 'leverage', or the use of aid to influence the policies of developing countries in one way or another, is necessary and desirable; and in developing countries that it is inevitable. The idea of leverage, as such, has not been much discussed.[14] But there has been much discussion of the desirability of particular development policies and numerous changes of view and fashion. In addition, the relevance of economic theories evolved in industrialized countries to the current problems of developing countries and the ability of Western-trained economists to solve them have been questioned.[15]

This study was based on the view that, if the idea of leverage was to be generally accepted by the supporters of

Series on International Economics and Development, 1966; Harry Magdoff, *The Age of Imperialism: The Economics of US Foreign Policy*, Monthly Review Press, 1969, chapter 4 on Aid and Trade; Edward S. Mason, *Foreign Aid and Foreign Policy*, New York, 1964, especially pp. 47–8; and forthcoming ODI study by Philip O'Brien, on the operations of US AID in Chile.

14. But see ODI publications cited in note 11. See also Manchester Conference on Teaching Economic Development, 1964, *The Teaching of Development Economics: Its Position in the Present State of Knowledge*, the proceedings, edited by Kurt Martin and John Knapp, Cass, 1967, especially paper by Dudley Seers, 'The Limitations of the Special Case'; *Towards a Strategy for Development Cooperation*, proceedings of a Conference on Asian Development, held by the Netherlands Economic Institute, Rotterdam University Press, 1967, *passim*; *Foreign Aid – A Critique and a Proposal*, Albert O. Hirschman and M. Bird, Essays in International Finance, No. 69, July 1968, Princeton University; and AID publications quoted in chapter 2, section on the AID, below.

15. See, for example, Manchester Conference on Teaching Economic Development, op. cit.; Gunnar Myrdal, *Asian Drama: An Inquiry into the Poverty of Nations*, 3 vols., Allen Lane The Penguin Press, 1968.

aid, it should be more carefully examined. As a contribution to the discussion, the study attempts to describe the activities of the World Bank, the IMF and the AID in Latin America.[16] Latin America is an area in which the issues emerge with particular force, for three main reasons: the relative complexity of the economies of Latin-American countries, the immediacy of their economic and financial problems and the particularly clear importance of political and social issues. The study is concerned solely with efforts to influence general economic policies and not, for example, with the World Bank's and the AID's project financing. From this, some conclusions emerged on the subject of leverage in general which differ considerably from, among other things, my own previous assumptions. These conclusions are set out in chapter 4. Chapter 2 describes the methods used by the IMF, the World Bank and the AID in influencing general economic policies in developing countries and the rationale for their involvement, and gives some indication of the policies they favour: it also describes briefly the role of the Inter-American Development Bank and the Inter-American Committee of the Alliance for Progress (CIAP), which are sometimes discussed in this connection, but whose influence is probably not as significant, and is certainly not as clearly perceived in Latin America, as that of the other three institutions. Chapter 3 describes the activities of the three major agencies, and their attitude towards policies, in the four countries I went to in the spring of 1967: Brazil, Chile, Colombia and Peru.

Because of the dearth of published material,[17] the study

16. For the reasons for concentrating on these three institutions and somewhat neglecting the other institutions of the Inter-American system, see chapter 2.

17. cf. also the Gruening Report, cited in this chapter, note 13, which says on p. vii of its Preface: 'Publications by international organiza-

has had to rely mainly on unpublished, and unquotable, written material, and above all on a large number of interviews with officials of the World Bank, the AID, the IMF, the Inter-American Development Bank (IADB, or BID), the United Nations Economic Commission for Latin America (CEPAL, or ECLA), the Inter-American Committee of the Alliance for Progress (CIAP) and Latin-American governments, and with politicians, academics, journalists, businessmen and so on, mainly in Brazil, Chile, Colombia, Peru and Washington, but also in Britain and, recently, in Cuba. Where quotation marks are used in the text, this usually means that a comment or statement made in one of these interviews is being repeated verbatim; attribution is naturally impossible, but it can be taken that the sources quoted are official and/or reliable and/or representative.

---

tions also were virtually useless. Filled with euphemisms in order not to offend anyone, they became so bland and obfuscated as to be virtually meaningless. Congressional hearings provided only a few tantalizing clues. . . . Thus, the bits and pieces from published sources furnished only fragmentary insights.'

Chapter 2

POLICIES, RATIONALE AND METHODS

THE concern of the World Bank and of the United States
AID with influencing macro-economic policies in Latin
America is fairly recent. They were preceded in this field by
the IMF. Involvement of the World Bank, the AID, and
the IMF has come about through differing processes and
their methods of trying to get their solutions adopted also
vary. Nevertheless the three institutions now work quite
closely together and there is, it is often said, 'a broad identity of views' between them. It is these institutions, and not
the others of the Inter-American system, which actually
conduct the negotiations with Latin-American governments
on general economic policies, and on linking the provision
of financial resources to the adoption of particular policies.

It is true that the idea of linking aid to 'performance'
was to some extent institutionalized and in theory multi-
lateralized in the framework of the Alliance for Progress,
after the Cuban revolution. The Charter of Punta del Este,
signed by the United States and all Latin-American governments except Cuba's in 1961, contained commitments by
the United States to provide higher levels of resources and
similar commitments by Latin-American governments to
invest resources, reform tax structures and land tenure
systems, and improve health, housing and education. The
Panel of Nine, which consisted of US and Latin-American
economists, was set up to review Latin-American development plans. In 1963 the Inter-American Economic and
Social Council (IA–ECOSOC) was reinforced by the
creation of the Inter-American Committee of the Alliance
for Progress (CIAP), 'for the purpose of representing

multilaterally the Alliance for Progress'. An attempt, in 1966, to absorb the Panel of Nine into the CIAP in order to control their activities resulted in the resignation of the Nine. But CIAP itself has quite strong Latin-American representation, and has shown a certain independence of view. CIAP conducts reviews of Latin-American governments' policies, and it is permitted to 'advise' on aid requirements and allocation. Agreements between the AID and Latin-American governments on 'aid and policy packages', embodied in Letters of Intent, are formally addressed to the CIAP. The World Bank, the Inter-American Development Bank (IADB, IDB, or BID), the AID and the IMF are regularly represented at CIAP meetings.

But CIAP, in spite of Latin-American efforts, was not given power to control the allocation of financial resources, including the United States aid theoretically provided under the Alliance for Progress. CIAP meetings, therefore, constitute little more than another channel of communication: at best, a forum in which an attempt may be made to reconcile the views of Latin-American governments and the major financial agencies. For all practical purposes, governments must deal directly with these agencies. The Inter-American Development Bank, in spite of the hopes expressed from time to time that it might promote the purposes of the Alliance for Progress, has so far shown itself unwilling to set 'general performance' as opposed to project conditions on the use of its resources; and such views as it does express on development policies are usually of a general and hortatory nature. Therefore the only institutions whose views on general economic policies are really likely to affect Latin American governments' access to aid are the World Bank, the AID, and the IMF.

A Latin-American government hoping to receive aid on

the basis of 'good performance' in economic matters will usually have to come to an agreement with the IMF. In some countries the World Bank and the AID rely on the IMF for an assessment of the government's performance, and merely add their weight to that of the IMF by making their support conditional on the country concerned reaching agreement with the IMF. The AID has, on occasion, specified to the government which of the IMF's conditions are important to it and which are not. The World Bank has claimed that it is acting as a mediator between the government and the Fund.[1] But in the cases where the World Bank and/or the AID do challenge the expertise of the IMF, or have views of their own on desirable macro-economic policies, the aim is increasingly that the three institutions should reach agreement together before negotiations are conducted with the government concerned. The IMF tends to be the main negotiator; but, according to the circumstances and the personalities involved, the nature of its demands may be the result of its own inclinations or of the pressure of one of the other institutions. The World Bank and the IMF, which share a building in Washington, and also publish a joint review, *Finance and Development*, have semi-formal arrangements for consultations on these issues.[2] Discussions have also taken place between the missions of the three institutions in the United States embassy in the country concerned.

Such co-operation is made easier by the fact that there is

1. See for example chapter 3, section on Colombia.
2. The World Bank's 1965-6 *Annual Report* mentions this (p. 7): 'The Bank and its sister organization, the International Monetary Fund, adopted a number of practices to extend still further their co-operation in obtaining, exchanging and evaluating economic information, and in advising their member-countries on matters of policy.' IMF officials also participate in the activities of the Bank's Economic Committee (see this chapter note 60). See also pp. 82-3 of this book.

a considerable measure of agreement between the three institutions on the policies which, in Latin America, they claim are crucial, and essential preconditions of development. Apart from the project-lending activities of the World Bank and the AID, all three institutions have concentrated primarily on 'performance' in the monetary and fiscal field with which the IMF has traditionally been concerned. Particular emphasis is laid on measures to achieve or maintain financial and monetary stability, and on the elimination of import and currency restrictions and price controls. A major goal, in spite of some demands for planning, especially of public sector investment, has been greater reliance on market mechanisms for achieving growth. But, above all, the agencies have been trying to persuade governments to adopt policies which they believe will bring about financial and monetary stability.

Such questions are at the heart of all negotiations, not only those with the IMF. They give rise to the 'key' conditions insisted upon by the international agencies. In Latin-American countries which do not have balance of payments problems and inflation, for example some Central American countries, and which do not have many controls, the international agencies are in general satisfied with existing policies, although the World Bank and the AID are sometimes also concerned with investment policies, taxation policies, and of course the financing of projects. In countries which do have such problems, the international agencies' first objective is usually to limit increases in the general level of demand. Budgetary deficits and excesses in credit creation are regarded as the primary causes of inflation. The IMF traditionally operates through control of the money supply. Governments are also expected to reduce their deficits on public account, preferably by reducing or limiting administrative expenditures and expenditures for 'non-productive' purposes and also by increasing revenues; if necessary by reducing public investment. Efforts are typically made to secure limitation of wage and salary increases in the public and private sectors and sometimes to secure the reduction of subsidies to public enterprises. Since the international agencies 'have had to live with' certain levels of inflation, they also frequently press for devaluation, as a means of controlling balance of payments deficits and also, it is hoped, of encouraging exports. Programmes also commonly include measures 'to eliminate price distortions', in particular by removing price controls on food, and, again, by devaluation. Frequently undertakings are required to remove or simplify controls on imports and capital movements, sometimes also to unify exchange rates or to reduce protection.[3]

The World Bank and the AID sometimes conduct separate negotiations for the adoption of particular policies, and the preoccupations of the three institutions do not, of course, always wholly converge. The World Bank,[4] pre-

3. See also Hirschman (*Foreign Aid – A Critique and a Proposal*, cited chapter 1, note 14), p. 6, e.g.: 'The commitment a country undertakes ... is typically of the following kind: to increase investment and decrease consumption, to increase the share of the private sector and decrease that of the public sector, to devalue the currency and thereby alter *relative* price relationships within the country, to throttle inflation and therefore strike a blow at the particular interest group whose turn it is to benefit from the next inflationary appropriation, credit expansion, or rise in prices or wages; and so on, and so forth.'

4. As one of the few published indications of the Bank's priorities, see the observations on judgeing performance published by the Bank in *Supplementary Financial Measures* (a study requested by the United Nations Conference on Trade and Development in 1964, published by the IBRD in December 1965). These end (p. 49) with the following suggestions: 'In some cases a series of simplified indicators could be used to assess country performance. These would mainly concentrate on a country's own efforts in resource mobilization and utilization and

sumably since it is itself engaged in financing projects in the public sector, is particularly interested in the level of public savings and in the quality and direction of the government's investment programme. It is concerned to ensure that the latter is financed by savings, rather than by short-term borrowing or by the printing of money. The Bank's current main criterion of performance is said to be 'the percentage of public investment financed from savings on current account'. The Bank is against large current government expenditures, especially on administration, but also in other 'non-productive' fields, such as housing. It is insistent on the financial viability of public enterprises, especially those to which it lends, and may demand that they should charge higher rates, or that they should dismiss some of their

---

on the results in growth. The following are illustrative of such indicators: ratio of tax revenues to GNP; ratio of public savings to total government revenues; ratio of total savings to GNP; ratio of total savings to GNP; ratio of "productive" investments (excluding non-essential public buildings, etc.) to GNP; rate of growth of GNP.' In a more recent Bank publication (*Some Aspects of the Economic Philosophy of the World Bank*, September 1968) Irving S. Friedman, after describing the common characteristics of the Bank and the Fund, says: 'Now, what are the differences between the Bank and the Fund? The most obvious difference is the question of priority when it comes to decision-making. In the Bank, our job is to do everything we can to accelerate economic growth and development. We have no other responsibility. And accelerating development, of course, comes down to questions of increasing productive capacity and increasing economic efficiency within the countries that are members of the World Bank. When we come to judge questions like performance ... our attitude is, and must be, that we judge a country's economic policy by its impact on investment, on savings, on growth – in short its impact on the development of the country. We must inform ourselves on the country's monetary policy, fiscal policy, exchange rates, investment programs, planning, foreign trade – all subjects that will arise in one way or another. We must always ask, what does this mean for the real economy? How will it work its way through the economy?' See also quotations pp. 58–63, below.

employees,[5] so that government subsidies to them can be reduced. The Bank is interested in the expansion and diversification of exports. In theory, its philosophy is more expansionist than that of the Fund, which is primarily concerned with balance (at whatever level), although there are examples of the Bank pressing as hard as, if not harder than, the Fund for deflationary policies.[6] The Bank is, finally, more interested than the Fund in the treatment of the private sector, especially foreign private investment, and it has a crucial interest in the government maintaining service payments on its external debt, both from its own point of view, as a past and future lender, and also because its Articles of Agreement enjoin it to support the flow of international investment.[7]

The AID, for its part, must show some concern for the adoption of reforms of the kind which the United States government committed itself to support under the Alliance for Progress. This concern is currently declining, but in the early sixties the AID was pressing for more progressive

5. The most notable example was in Argentina, where in 1967 the World Bank was insisting, as a condition for its support, that 70,000 people should be dismissed from the railways.

6. As can be seen from a comparison of the 1966 Bank and Fund Reports on Chile. The Bank was also, both in Peru and in Colombia, more convinced than the Fund of the necessity of devaluation.

7. There is an internal Bank document entitled *Policy Memorandum 204* which states that the Bank shall not lend to countries which default on debt repayments or servicing (without agreeing on re-financing), which nationalize foreign-owned assets (without adequate compensation), or which fail to honour agreements with foreign private investors (for example tax agreements). This Memorandum has been invoked, for example, against Egypt, Burma, Ceylon, Iraq, Indonesia, Brazil, Costa Rica and Guatemala (although the Bank usually also had other reasons for being unwilling to lend to these countries), and is currently being invoked in Peru over the issue of the nationalization of some long-disputed assets of the United States International Petroleum Company.

31

systems of taxation, for land reform, and so on. Some vestiges of this concern remain, especially in the field of education; but they are not central to the AID's demands. The AID is also particularly interested in programmes of import liberalization, although it has, on occasion, discouraged the removal of exchange controls, since this makes it difficult to ensure that US aid is used for imports from the US. In addition, the AID often has to press the interests of particular United States firms established in the country concerned, of United States exporters, or of firms established in the United States whose markets a developing country is threatening to invade.[8] In countries where, for 'security' reasons, the United States government wants to support a particular government, the AID will be expected to be more lenient in its judgement of good performance than it might otherwise be; the IMF and possibly the World Bank may also be persuaded to demand less as a condition of their support.

But, political considerations of this nature aside, there is a 'broad identity of views' on the main aspects of 'good performance' in Latin America. The international agencies explain their present priorities by pointing to the urgency and immediacy of most Latin-American countries' problems of inflation, balance of payments deficits and debts. They argue that these problems must be solved first, and that thereafter more attention can be paid to other issues, including long-term development. Meanwhile their role, as they see it, is to ensure that the existing system continues to function, that major crises are avoided, and, especially in the case of the World Bank, that debts can be repaid. They sometimes also argue that other issues, especially issues of

8. For example the threat of cutting aid was used in the dispute over Brazil's exports of soluble coffee, which were taking a large share of the US market.

a social and political nature, and especially the problems created for Latin-American countries by the decline in their terms of trade in the fifties and sixties, are outside the scope and competence of the international agencies and difficult for them to influence. There is the additional difficulty of reducing social and political objectives to specific and quantifiable targets.[9]

In the rest of this chapter an attempt is made to describe the history, rationale and methods of the involvement in general policies of the three institutions separately. There are also short sections describing the role and attitudes of the Inter-American Development Bank and the CIAP.

THE INTERNATIONAL MONETARY FUND

Of the three major international agencies, the IMF, in attempting to influence the policies of its members, is fulfilling a role which is most clearly provided for in its statutes and is most formalized. On the other hand the IMF's policies have evolved considerably since it was first set up, and to some extent its priorities are different from those intended at Bretton Woods, at least by Britain and some other countries. Moreover the IMF was not set up with the developing countries in mind and it was not foreseen that

9. Hirschman (in *Foreign Aid – A Critique and a Proposal*, cited chapter 1, note 14) has another explanation: 'The fact that certain commitments have less latitude in implementation and are therefore less prone to sabotage than others has naturally led to a preference of aid negotiators for these types of commitments. In this way we can explain the increasing tendency to make programme aid depend on the taking of specific monetary and exchange-rate measures and on the "appropriate" behaviour of certain fiscal and monetary indicators, while less and less attention is paid to economic growth and social justice, supposedly the principal objectives of aid.'

it would become so deeply involved in the policies of non-industrialized countries, especially those in Latin America.

The Fund was primarily intended to promote orderly exchange conditions, especially among the North Atlantic countries who had suffered from the lack of such order in the 1930s. Its Articles of Agreement state that the Fund's purposes are to promote international monetary co-operation; to facilitate the expansion of international trade and thus to contribute to the maintenance of high levels of employment and income; to promote exchange stability, maintain orderly exchange arrangements, and avoid competitive depreciation of exchange rates; to assist in the multilateralization of payments and in the elimination of foreign exchange restrictions on current transactions; and to make its resources available under adequate safeguards so that balance of payments disequilibria can be corrected without inducing recessions.

The Fund's resources are provided through its members' subscriptions, based on quotas initially negotiated at Bretton Woods. The size of the quotas was determined mainly by the size of members' reserves and national income and their dependence on foreign trade, and also, to some extent, by political considerations. At the time of Bretton Woods the resources thus made available amounted to $8,800 million. By 1968, after a 50 per cent all-round increase in quotas, the addition of new members and some adjustments of individual quotas, they amounted to $21,100 million. Each member was expected to pay in 25 per cent of its quota (or 10 per cent of the value of its reserves, if this was less) in gold, and the rest in its own currency. Members are expected to repurchase their currencies, or 'repay' the IMF's loans of currencies, usually in three to five years.[10] The Articles of Agreement

10. See IMF *Annual Report* for 1952.

lay down progressive charges on these drawings, intended to ensure that the use of the Fund's resources is temporary, starting at 0·5 per cent and increasing over time up to 5 per cent, before which point the member is expected to consult with the Fund on the reduction of the Fund's holdings of its currency. Since 1953, the Fund has been able to make 'stand-by arrangements', under which it is agreed that a country can make drawings from the Fund, when and if it needs to, up to a stated amount over a stated period, usually one year, without negotiating new agreements with the Fund.

Voting rights of Members of the Fund are determined by the size of their quotas. The Articles of Agreement state that the Fund shall be headed by a Board of Governors each of whom represents a member government, and by Executive Directors selected by members, five of them appointed by the five members with the largest quotas, one appointed by a country with a surplus in its balance of payments, and the remaining seven elected by groups of members not entitled to appoint directors. Voting power in these two groups is, in general, in proportion to the size of members' quotas; in decisions on members' access to the Fund's resources, the voting is further weighted in favour of surplus countries.[11] In practice, the Executive Directors have taken a considerable interest in the day-to-day working of the Fund and are consulted on most issues. The system of weighted voting, together with the fact that the Fund is located in Washington, has meant that the objectives of the major economic powers, and of the United States in particular, have been closely reflected in the Fund's activities.

Keynes's original idea of a Clearing Union, providing automatic access to resources in effect three or four times

11. See IMF *Annual Reports* for the subscriptions and voting power of members.

the size of those agreed for the IMF at Bretton Woods, and with supervisory powers of a technical nature only in the field of exchange rates, was abandoned at an early stage of the negotiations. Not only were the Fund's resources to be smaller and provided in a manner which made it more difficult to increase them,[12] but access to them was made subject to a number of conditions under the Articles of Agreement. One in particular, stated in Article V, section 5, allows wide interpretation: 'Whenever the Fund is of the opinion that any member is using the resources of the Fund in a manner contrary to the purposes of the Fund, it shall present to the member a report setting forth the views of the Fund and prescribing a suitable time for reply. After presenting such a report to a member, the Fund may limit the use of its resources by the member. If no reply to the report is received from the member within the prescribed time, or if the reply received is unsatisfactory, the Fund may continue to limit the member's use of the Fund's resources or may, after giving reasonable notice to the member, declare it ineligible to use the resources of the Fund.'[13]

On the question of exchange rates, the Articles of Agreement made clear that exchange rates should be fixed in the short-term, but could be varied from time to time to adjust to price changes and to help to prevent balance of payments disequilibrium. Under Article IV, members of the IMF may not change the parity of their currency by more than 10 per cent of the initial par value agreed with the Fund without consulting with the Fund and in any case should not propose

12. The Keynes proposal was that the Clearing Union's resources should be in the nature of overdraft facilities, an increase in whose ceilings would have been easier to agree than an increase in subscriptions.

13. See also Article VI, on Capital Transfers, Article VII, on Scarce Currencies, and below.

a change except to correct a 'fundamental disequilibrium'. In practice the Fund has used its discretion in actively trying to promote changes in exchange rates, especially in Latin America.[14]

In addition, members of the Fund, under Article VIII, are expected to avoid restrictions on current payments, to avoid discriminatory currency arrangements or multiple currency practices and to maintain convertibility on current account. They are expected to provide information to the Fund when asked to do so on these and other questions: for example, their official holdings of gold and foreign exchange, balance of payments, national income, and internal price movements. It was accepted that, in theory in the immediate post-war period, most countries would be unable to comply with the provisions of Article VIII.[15]

Therefore, under Article XIV, countries were permitted, for a 'transitional period', to maintain exchange restrictions and multiple currency practices. From 1952 any countries retaining such restrictions have been obliged periodically to 'consult' with the Fund; usually such consultations take place every year. The Fund is entitled to recommend in its Report to the Directors that a country give up its restrictions and can, if the country fails to comply with IMF recommendations, declare it ineligible to use the Fund's resources and eventually require it to withdraw from Fund membership. The procedure of consultations applies whether or not a country has an

14. Although it has also been argued that the Fund could have used its powers in this field more positively, especially in the post-war years in Europe. cf. W. M. Scammel, *International Monetary Policy*, second edition, Macmillan, 1961, p. 187.

15. At first the only countries which declared themselves able to do so were El Salvador, Guatemala, Mexico, Panama and the United States.

immediate need for financial support from the Fund. Most developing countries are still subject to the provisions of Article XIV.

In spite of the insertion of these conditions, the Articles of Agreement do not in themselves provide a clear basis for the Fund's subsequent involvement in the domestic policies of its members. The British view of the function of the Fund was partly incorporated in the Articles of Agreement, and was basically that the Fund should provide its members with more or less automatic access to its resources to help them to deal with their balance of payments problems without resorting to severe deflation, and that the Fund should have no direct influence or control over the national policies of members. The United States view was that the Fund should exercise control and scrutiny over all drawings and should have discretion to promote what it considered to be appropriate domestic policies in its member countries.[16] In 1946 a declaration was made, in response to a request for 'information' from the Board of Governors, that: 'The Executive Directors of the IMF interpret the Articles of Agreement to mean that authority to use the resources of the Fund is limited to use in accordance with its purposes to give temporary assistance in financing balance of payments deficits on current account for monetary stabilization operations.'[17] The Fund, clearly promoting the United States' point of view, began to see its major objective not as the provision of additional international liquidity freely available to members, but as the achievement of the multilateralization of trade and the elimination

16. See for example Professor R. F. Harrod, *The Life of John Maynard Keynes*, Macmillan, 1951, and W. M. Scammel, *International Monetary Policy*, second edition, Macmillan, 1961.

17. *Report of the Executive Directors and Summary Proceedings*, 27 September–3 October 1946, p. 106.

of currency restrictions.[18] From 1949 it published *Annual Reports* on Exchange Restrictions, and it began actively pressing its members to eliminate restrictions and multiple exchange rates.

From the early fifties the Fund made it increasingly clear that the use of its resources should be regarded as a means of meeting temporary balance of payments difficulties through *conditional* short-term advances. Its concern with members' domestic policies grew, particularly with those policies considered likely to promote inflation, such as large investment or social security programmes. In 1951 Mr Ivor Booth, the Fund's Managing Director, informed members that the Fund's resources would be available only on certain conditions, that members should adopt programmes to control inflation and that they should reduce restrictions on trade.[19] It was later[20] made plain that, although the Fund would be unlikely to refuse permission for drawings equal to a member's gold subscription (the 'gold *tranche*' or first 25 per cent of its quota), drawings on

18. See Scammel, op. cit., p. 163: 'To [the IMF's] provisions for the re-establishment of multilateral trade the North Americans attached great importance believing such re-establishment to be a main *raison d'être* of the Fund. ... The virtual aloofness of the Fund from postwar balance of payments problems, the passing into other hands of the measures designed to deal with these, and the dominance of American opinion in the formation of Fund policy tended to shift the emphasis of the Fund's purpose from that originally intended at Bretton Woods and place it upon this liberalising mission.'

19. See Address to the Annual Meeting of the Board of Governors, September 1951. This statement coincided with US demands for anti-inflationary policies in Western Europe. See also the Fund's fourth Annual Report on Exchange Restrictions, 1953, which stated: 'Where certain countries tended to alternate between more extensive use of restrictions and more reliance on corrective monetary and fiscal measures, the Fund made clear the desirability of the latter type.'

20. See *Annual Report* for 1955.

subsequent *tranches* would carry progressively stricter conditions. More recently the Fund has usually required members wishing to make drawings from the Fund or stand-by arrangements to provide a Letter of Intent, stating in some detail the policies it intends to adopt. In the case of a stand-by arrangement, the member may make a drawing from the Fund only if the Fund considers that it has complied with the conditions in the Letter of Intent.[21]

The Fund's activities and pressures have been concentrated in Europe, and its first concern, as has been said, is with the smooth functioning of monetary relationships between the major economic powers of the North Atlantic. It nevertheless became involved in Latin America at an early stage. Latin-American countries were 'some of the worst offenders' in multiple currency practices. They also suffered particularly acutely from balance of payments problems and inflation, especially in the fifties during the period of rapidly falling primary commodity prices. Some governments came to the IMF simply for advice, without necessarily asking for drawings from the Fund. The majority of the Fund's stand-by arrangements have been in Latin America. Although Fund reports on countries subject

21. Since 1963 the Fund has been able to provide financial support in a third form, that of Compensatory Finance for short-term export fluctuations. This support is based on calculations of weighted average export earnings in the current and two preceding years and of a five year average including projections for the likely values of major commodities in the next two years. Although it is thus based on a fairly technical evaluation, the notion of automatic disbursement is explicitly rejected. (See IMF, *Compensatory Financing of Export Fluctuations,* Washington D.C., February 1963, pp. 9–14). The decision whether to provide Compensatory Finance in given circumstances remains at the discretion of the Fund. As a result of the necessity of statistical evaluation, drawings occur after a time lag, by which time a country with no reserves may have failed to meet other IMF conditions and have forfeited IMF support. (See for example chapter 3, section on Colombia.)

to Article XIV still conclude formally with a recommendation that the country be permitted to maintain specified exchange restrictions and perhaps a statement that others are to be abandoned, the reports have become increasingly comprehensive. They are intended, as Fund officials put it, to 'help countries maintain a stable monetary situation.' Governments wanting to use the resources of the Fund must now agree to a programme of specific measures designed to achieve financial and monetary stability which is generally embodied in a Letter of Intent addressed to the Executive Directors, who are closely concerned in decisions on the use of the Fund's resources. The inducement for governments to come to the Fund has been increased in recent years by the policy of the World Bank and the AID of making their support conditional on agreement with the Fund. The Fund's approval of Latin-American governments may also be a condition for their access to other forms of finance, official and private. The Fund has been influential in debt re-scheduling operations.[22] No doubt also governments with serious economic and political problems find it tempting to turn them over to the IMF and the rest of the international community and blame them for any resulting unpleasantness. Finally the desire of Latin-American governments to remain in good international standing is quite widespread.

At any rate, in the fifties and sixties there have been numerous IMF 'stabilization programmes' in Latin America. They have become the subject of considerable controversy. Although the Fund publishes neither its Reports nor the Letters of Intent addressed to it, it is well known that these exist and there is therefore some idea of what they contain; some of them have also been published or

22. For example for Brazil in 1961 and 1965; for Argentina in 1962 and 1965; for Chile in 1965.

made available, in the countries concerned. Moreover the Fund has published, in its *Staff Papers*, and in its review published jointly with the World Bank, *Finance and Development*, articles which can be taken to represent its attitude on stabilization policies.[23] There have also been a number of accounts of I M F programmes published by outsiders; these usually argue that the I M F's exigencies have depressive effects on employment and production, without achieving long-run stability.[24]

23. See for example J. J. Polak, 'Have economists said their final word in the fight against inflation?', *Finance and Development*, No. 3, 1968; U Tun Wai, 'The Relation between Inflation and Economic Development: A Statistical Inductive Study', *IMF Staff Papers*, Vol. VII (1959–60); I. Bhatia, 'Inflation, Deflation and Economic Development', *IMF Staff Papers*, Vol. VIII (1960–61); Gertrud Lovasy, 'Inflation and Exports in Primary Producing Countries', *IMF Staff Papers*, Vol. IX, No. 1, March 1962; A. S. Shaalan, 'The Impact of Inflation on the Composition of Private Domestic Investment' *IMF Staff Papers*, Vol. IX, No. 2, July 1962; Graeme Dorrance, 'The Effect of Inflation on Economic Development', *IMF Staff Papers*, Vol. X, No. 1, March 1962, and 'Inflation and Growth: the Statistical Evidence', *IMF Staff Papers*, Vol. XIII, No. 1, March 1966; Hannan Ezekiel, 'Monetary Expansion and Economic Development', *IMF Staff Papers*, Vol. XIV, No. 1, March 1967; Ernest Sturc, 'Stabilization Policies: Experience of Some European Countries in the 1950's', *IMF Staff Papers*, Vol. XV, No. 2, July 1968; and S. Kanesa-Thasan, 'Stabilizing an Economy – A Study of the Republic of Korea', *IMF Staff Papers*, Vol. XVI, No. 1, March 1969.

24. Some of the main opponents of Fund policies in Latin America have been a school of economists, mainly in the United Nations Economic Commission for Latin America (ECLA or CEPAL), who came to be known as 'structuralists'. Structuralists usually argue that deflationary policies of the IMF or 'monetarist' variety do not eliminate the fundamental causes of inflation, that it is necessary to make structural changes, including some expansion and reorientation of production and some redistribution of income, if stability is to be achieved, and that two of the major causes of inflation are the slow growth of food supplies, due largely to rigid systems of land tenure,

The scope of the Fund's programmes extends well beyond anything envisaged in the IMF's Articles of Agreement. One of the earliest extensions of Fund concern was in the field of Central Bank credit policies, whose control was, and is, regarded as one of the main ways of dealing with balance of payments problems. Fund programmes also go increasingly into the details of fiscal policy, wages policy, even occasionally agricultural policy, as well as emphasizing the Fund's traditional concern with exchange rates and exchange restrictions. The Fund argues that financial and monetary stability cannot be secured without attention to such issues. It has also, in recent years, claimed that it is

and of exports, due largely to the slow growth of demand for primary products. (See also pp. 163–4) There is a large literature on structuralism and on the structuralist–monetarist controversy. See for example: A. O. Hirschman (ed.), *Latin American Issues, Essays and Comments*, The Twentieth Century Fund, New York, 1961, especially sections by Roberto Campos, David Felix and Joseph Grunwald; Dudley Seers, 'A Theory of Inflation in Under-Developed Countries Based on the Experience of Latin America', *Oxford Economic Papers*, June 1962; Dr Raul Prebisch, 'Economic Development or Monetary Stability – The False Dilemma', *UN Economic Bulletin for Latin America*, March 1961; ECLA, 'Inflation and Growth, A Summary of Experience in Latin America', *UN Economic Bulletin for Latin America*, February 1962; Osvaldo Sunkel, 'Inflation in Chile: An Unorthodox Approach', *International Economic Papers*, No. 10 (also in *El Trimestre Económico*, octubre–diciembre 1958), and 'El Fracaso de las Políticas de Estabilización', *El Trimestre Económico*, octubre–diciembre 1963; David Felix, 'Structural Imbalances, Social Conflict and Inflation: an appraisal of Chile's recent anti-inflationary effort', *Economic Development and Cultural Change*, January 1960; Aníbal Pinto, *Chile – Un Caso de Desarrollo Frustrado*, Collección América Nuestra, Editorial Universitaria S.A., Santiago de Chile, 1962 (pp. 125–47), and *Chile – Una Economía Difícil*, Central CEPAL–BNDE, 1964 (pp. 60–81); and Werner Baer in *Latin American Research Review*, spring 1967. See also Martin L. Loftus, 'The International Monetary Fund 1955–67: A Selected Bibliography', *IMF Staff Papers*, March 1968; and chapter 4, notes 3 and 14.

concerned with the problems of development as such. Partly as a result of the widespread criticism of the effects of Fund stabilization programmes on Latin-American economies, the Fund has tended to argue not merely that its policies will achieve stabilization, but that such stabilization is an essential precondition of development.[25] Officials are more willing than they were in the past to recognize that their short-term exigencies can have adverse effects on long-term policies and that they ought to take these effects into account in the demands they make on countries wanting to use the Fund's resources. There has moreover been some limited acceptance of 'structuralist' arguments[26] on the importance of supply bottlenecks in the problems of inflation, and the Fund is more concerned than in the past with levels of production and with government activities.

Nevertheless the Fund, as one official put it, is interested in development 'at one step removed'. As an example, it was said that the Fund's interest in increasing governments' revenues from taxation, in so far as it has such an interest, was a result of the Fund's inability to secure reductions in

25. For example Graeme Dorrance (in 'The Effect of Inflation on Economic Development', *IMF Staff Papers*, Vol. X, No. 1, March 1962, under the subtitle 'Inflation is Not the Only Problem of Development') has the following paragraph: 'The control of inflation is only one of the problems facing a government wishing to encourage rapid economic development. The fight against illiteracy, the reform of bureaucratic practices, the building of basic sanitary facilities for the eradication of endemic diseases, the substitution of competitive for monopolistic trade practices, the encouragement of a widespread spirit of entrepreneurship, and the creation of an adequate amount of social capital, may be important prerequisites for rapid growth. However, attacks on these problems are likely to be more feasible in an atmosphere of financial stability: a rapid inflation will make the failure of such attacks much more likely.'

26. See this chapter, note 24, and chapter 4, section on Alternative Policies in Latin America (i).

their spending. Moreover when the Fund permits policies of an expansionist nature it is sometimes said to be making 'concessions'. In other words, concessions to Latin-American countries' desire and need to promote rapid development even though, in the Fund's view, this will mean higher rates of inflation and therefore greater instability in the balance of payments and exchange rates and probably a need to retain or intensify exchange restrictions.

There is thus a potential conflict between the Fund's purposes, especially as interpreted by the United States, and the objective of development. The Fund's attempt to reconcile this conflict by arguing that financial and monetary stability are a precondition of development is a somewhat artificial one. Like the British at Bretton Woods and afterwards, Latin Americans could answer that the purpose of the Fund should be to make resources freely available to enable them to solve their balance of payments problems *without* resorting to severely deflationary policies, at least of the sort advocated by the IMF. It can be claimed that the Fund, more than in the past, takes into account the requirements of development. But it should not be claimed, as it sometimes is, that these are of vital concern to the Fund, or in any sense have priority in its operations. It can on the contrary be asserted, given the international purposes of the Fund and the biased nature of its government, that the interests of the developing countries, where they conflict with those of the developed countries, will regularly be sacrificed.

From the beginning the United States showed a determination to use the Fund to promote its own objectives: non-discrimination against United States exports, the removal of restrictions on trade, stable exchange rates and the control of inflation. It seems that the attitude of the present surplus countries in Europe is now at least as militant as that of the United States on the need for anti-inflationary policies. The promotion of such objectives, if it is true that they are necessary to ensure the smooth functioning of the international system and to avoid crises leading to more severe deflation and reduction in levels of trade, can be said to be indirectly beneficial to all members of the Fund. But for the developing countries the smooth functioning of the system is only beneficial to the extent that the system is beneficial to them; and this, if one is to judge both by the circumstances of unequal power in which the system has evolved and by the developing countries' present situation, is not very far. From their point of view, therefore, what matters is the direct effect of Fund policies on their individual prospects of development.[27]

THE WORLD BANK

The World Bank is an institution whose major and best-known activity has been to contribute to the financing of projects.[28] The Bank's ideas about influencing the general economic policies of developing countries, and its methods of doing so, are still at a formative stage. They have not been generalized or formalized and they were not envisaged in the Bank's original statutes. They are also very little known to the general public. They are nevertheless increasingly important.

The International Bank for Reconstruction and Develop-

27. See chapter 4.
28. The projects are not the subject of this study. For a descriptive account of the World Bank Group, see for example a document published by the Group: *The World Bank, IDA and IFC, Policies and Operations*, April 1968.

ment (IBRD, or World Bank) was set up at Bretton Woods to complement the activities of the IMF by promoting a steady flow of international investment for the development of productive resources. It was thought that the Bank would thus contribute to international stability and, by sharing risks, would ensure that surplus countries would fulfil their 'investment function'. The Bank's Articles of Agreement state that the purposes of the Bank are to assist in post-war reconstruction by facilitating investment; to promote private foreign investment by means of guarantees and participations and if necessary to supplement this investment by providing finance for productive purposes out of its own capital, funds raised by it and its other resources; to promote trade and balance of payments equilibrium by encouraging international investment for the development of productive resources; to ensure that priority projects are dealt with first; and to conduct its operations with due regard to the effect of international investment on business conditions in its members' territories.

The Bank's membership is the same as that of the IMF. Its members initially subscribed $10,000 million to the capital of the Bank, in proportion to quotas, most of which are equal to their quotas in the Fund. The Bank's quotas were doubled in 1959 at the same time as the Fund's quotas were increased. The original subscriptions to the Bank's capital were in three parts: 2 per cent was payable in gold or US dollars and freely available for lending; 18 per cent was payable in members' own currency and called up subsequently, with members' consent; the remaining 80 per cent is not available for lending but is subject to call if required to honour guarantees or to meet defaults. All of the 1959 increase in subscriptions was to remain subject to call. The Bank has not in fact operated through providing guarantees for private lenders.[29] It has made loans from its own resources, from its subscribed capital and by raising money in its own name in private capital markets; and it has also sold participations in its own loans to private investors. Of the Bank's total $9,985 million of funds available for lending up to June 1968, $1,906 million was accounted for by usable subscriptions, $5,667 million by borrowings and sales of loans, $1,500 million by repayments of principal, and $912 million by income from the Bank's operations.[30] By June 1968, the Bank had made loans totalling $7,234 million. Bank loans are long term, usually with maturities of 15–25 years; interest on them was raised in August 1968 to 6½ per cent. Since 1962, through the International Development Association (IDA), the Bank has been able to make loans on softer terms; IDA loans are repayable in 50 years and carry a service charge of 0·75 per cent. Loans from the IDA are administered in the same way as loans from the Bank's ordinary resources and used for very much the same purposes; decisions on whether to lend from IDA resources are based on the economic situation of the country as a whole, and on its capacity to service debts, rather than on the nature of particular projects.

The proceeds of the Bank's loans, either from its ordinary resources or through the IDA, may be spent in any of its member countries. The Articles of Agreement stipulate that they shall be available, except in 'exceptional circumstances', only for projects approved by the Bank, and only for the direct foreign exchange costs of such projects. The Bank, in 1947, in its function as a bank for reconstruction, made some 'programme loans' to European countries and recently it has made a few such loans, for specified groups

29. Except through the IFC, set up in 1959.

30. *World Bank, International Development Association, Annual Report, 1968*, p. 25.

of commodities, to India and Pakistan. It has also stated that if necessary it is prepared to finance the indirect foreign exchange costs of projects.[31] All Bank loans must be made to governments or have government guarantees. The Bank has in fact done little, directly, to promote productive investment in the private sector, although it has lent, with government guarantees, to some private development banks, to private railway companies, electric power companies, and so on. More recently it has lent to some commercial undertakings in the agricultural sector; it has also, in a general sense, been very much concerned with the encouragement of foreign private investment and with its treatment by national governments.[32] The majority of Bank loans have been in the public sector and usually in the economic infrastructure. The Bank's function in reconstruction has ended and it is now primarily an institution concerned with the development of the less-developed countries. In the years 1965–8, however, loans were signed for Spain, Portugal, Greece, South Africa, New Zealand, Iceland, Israel and Japan.[33]

The Bank's government is similar to that of the Fund. It has a Board of Governors, each of them representing a member, and twelve Executive Directors, five appointed by

31. The Articles of Agreement state that 'in exceptional circumstances' Bank loans may cover part of the local currency costs or the indirect foreign exchange costs of the projects for which the Bank is lending (Article IV, section 3, b, c and d).

32. The Bank's Articles of Agreement contain only the general injunctions in Article I on the subject of private investment (see p. 47). But a subsequent decision by the Governors established that the Bank may not lend to countries whose treatment of foreign private investment is considered unsatisfactory (see this chapter, note 7); and Bank reports contain injunctions on this subject (see, for example, pp. 138–9, in section on Brazil).

33. See *Annual Reports* for 1965–6, 1966–7, and 1968.

the five members with the largest quotas and seven elected by the remaining members. Voting power is in proportion to the size of quotas. Thus the United States, in 1968, had 25·92 per cent of the voting power, Britain 10·73 per cent.[34]

From the beginning, the Bank made considerable efforts to ensure that its projects were priority ones, and its procedures for negotiating loans are complicated and protracted. In its *Annual Report* for 1949–50, the Bank stated: 'To be of maximum effectiveness Bank investment must be devoted to those undertakings which will contribute most to strengthening the economy of the borrowing country.' Subsequent Reports described in some detail the Bank's methods of selecting and negotiating projects and the criteria on which choice is based. The Bank has increasingly attached to its loans conditions designed to increase the viability of projects, and the field covered by these conditions has been extended. An important part of the Bank's project-lending has been an effort to improve the organization of the institutions responsible for administering Bank projects: railway authorities, electricity companies and so on. Especially in Latin America the Bank has also made considerable efforts to increase the financial viability of the public and private enterprises to which it makes its loans, in particular by persuading governments to allow them to charge higher rates for their services; and it has generally insisted, at the time when it makes its loans, that the rates charged fully cover the costs of the projects. The Bank has had some influence on project choice, insisting for example that countries should start projects which, in the Bank's view, could be completed; and it has been very insistent on thorough preparation, feasibility studies and the use of consultants. In addition, the range of sectors in which the

34. See *Annual Reports* for members' subscriptions and voting rights.

Bank is prepared to finance projects has been enlarged. The Bank is now putting some emphasis on the need to finance projects in agriculture and education, sectors which were originally thought unsuitable for a banking institution; the fact that it has, in practice, been slow in starting on such projects demonstrates the difficulty experienced by the Bank in moving from its traditional concentration on 'safe' projects, with a minimum of social implications and complications.

But, in addition to its project-lending policies, the Bank has also become concerned with the general economic policies of the countries to which it lends. It is said that, in principle, the Bank must now approve both the project and the country before it decides to make a loan. The Bank has not stated clearly and publicly that this is so. Its *Annual Reports* refer to the fact that it has for some time produced reports on countries' general development policies. But the purpose of these reports is stated to be to enable it to improve its policies in the selection of projects, not to serve as the basis for setting 'general performance' conditions before giving financial support; and, since the reports are no longer intended for publication,[35] it is also hard to discover what the Bank's views on development policies are. Addresses to the Board of Governors by Presidents of the Bank contain references to general development policies, and brief comments on these policies, but do not refer to leverage.[36] The Bank's *Annual Reports* are similarly

35. In the fifties and early sixties the Bank published a number of general country reports, in the Johns Hopkins Press; but these cannot be taken as representative of the Bank's views on development. (See pp. 65–6.)

36. For example, Mr McNamara's Address to the Boards of Governors, 30 September 1968, emphasized the need for birth-control programmes, and the Bank's willingness to assist with such programmes, but did not mention any conditionality.

unforthcoming. For the first time, in 1968, the Bank's *Annual Report* specifically referred to the fact that it is making its lending conditional on the adoption of general policies it considers satisfactory, when it stated:

... the need to make most effective possible use of the resources available for development has been constantly stressed by the Bank over the years and is its guiding principle in its relationship with borrowing countries. The performance by a country in the promotion of its economic development is an important criterion for financial assistance from the Bank or IDA.[37]

And further on, the Bank provided some limited elaboration of this statement:

To provide the general framework within which financing activities are conducted, the Bank seeks to acquire a comprehensive picture of the position and prospects of borrowing countries' economies and their development requirements. This makes it possible to identify sectors and areas of high potential and provides guidelines to the types of projects which should be given early attention. It also enables judgements to be formed about a country's economic policies and other questions relevant to its economic growth and to its eligibility for Bank or IDA financing.

The Bank's economic analysis is a continuous process, based on work at Head Office, visits to borrowing countries to gain first hand knowledge of their economies, and frequent contacts with government and other officials. By giving continuous attention to the economic situation of developing countries in this way, the Bank hopes to help them make more effective use of the resources at their disposal and so accelerate their rate of progress. Among the principal matters with which the Bank assists member countries are the formulation of development policies, the establishment of development organizations, the drawing up of investment programmes for specific sectors and

37. *World Bank, International Development Association, Annual Report, 1968*, p. 7.

regions, and the identification and preparation of projects for financing.[38]

Nowhere else in recent Bank *Annual Reports* is there any specific mention of general conditions on bank lending, although under the two customary headings of 'Co-ordination' and 'Technical Assistance'[39] there are numerous references to the Bank's advice on, and study of, general development issues. Some clues on the Bank's attitude are to be found. For example the 1966–7 *Annual Report* is prefaced by a quotation from a speech by the Bank's President, Mr George Woods, which ends with the obviously carefully-worded paragraph:

We early concluded that any developing country would benefit from having some kind of programme as a framework for development, relating projects to each other, taking account of the availability of financial resources, and giving thought to policy and administrative measures as well as to physical projects that would accelerate economic development. We have therefore developed a practice of organizing expert missions to visit individual countries and to draw up comprehensive recommendations that serve as a basis for working out a detailed development programme. What we want, in a word, is to encourage constantly improving economic performance by our developing member countries. Not every country can have, or even profit from, a detailed development programme, but every country can aspire to a well thought-out set of policies which will provide the conditions and motivations conducive to economic growth. This is more and more what we find ourselves talking about with our member countries – fundamental policies to

38. ibid., p. 8.

39. These sections are primarily concerned with consortia and consultative groups, whose activities and policies are relatively fully described. See also John White, *Pledged to Development*, ODI, 1967; and Michael Hoffman (of the World Bank Staff), 'The Coordination of Aid', in *Effective Aid*, ODI, 1966.

govern their day-to-day economic decisions. We are able to talk about policies and policy changes not as interlopers but as collaborators – and sometimes we give agreed policies the final measure of support they need to tip the scales in their favour in the councils of government.

Later in the same *Annual Report* (p. 6) under the heading 'Coordinating Development Assistance', the Bank argues its suitability for such activities:

As multilateral institutions with a broad mandate from member governments, the World Bank Group has certain advantages in the administration of development finance. The member governments of the Bank are also its shareholders, and this circumstance creates the possibility of an unusually close and co-operative relationship between the Bank Group and the developing countries. After 21 years of operations and with an international staff chosen strictly on professional merits, the Group has acquired special experience and expertise in the development field. It has no political, commercial or other non-developmental objectives to distract it from its function of assisting the economic growth of its developing member countries. In providing external finance for projects of high economic priority, and in offering advice on a wide range of development problems in the less developed countries, the Bank Group may help bring about a more effective use of domestic resources and of assistance made available under bilateral programmes.

Another published statement by the Bank, which can be taken to express its views on these issues, although it does not deal with the Bank's own lending policies, is the Bank's report to UNCTAD on Supplementary Financial Measures (SFM).[40] It is worth quoting from this Report, since it describes the role which might be played by an 'Agency'

40. *Supplementary Financial Measures: A Study Requested by the United Nations Conference on Trade and Development – 1964*, published by the IBRD in December 1965.

which was intended to be the Bank itself and since it has been stated, privately but authoritatively, that the description of the conditions on which the Agency would release its resources reflects the current practice of the Bank with respect to its own lending decisions. For example, the Report proposes that Supplementary Finance, 'to deal with problems arising from adverse movements in [developing countries'] export proceeds', should be available on condition that:

(i) prior to the shortfall, the member consulted with the Agency to reach a common understanding regarding the export projection and the 'policy package' underlying it;

(ii) during the interval between consultation and the shortfall the Agency did not inform the member that it could not rely on help from the Scheme because it was disregarding agreed policies; and

(iii) actual exports fell below projected exports and the size of the shortfall exceeded previous averages during the current projection period.[41]

The first two conditions correspond to the Bank's practice of trying to agree on 'policy packages' and aid requirements, and supervising the execution of policies, with its potential borrowers. In addition the Report proposes that assistance from the Agency should be available if it can be shown that export shortfalls have caused 'disruption of development programmes'; the purpose of this criterion, it is said, 'is to make sure that the Scheme satisfies a developmental need rather than some notion of equity or other objectives, however laudable.' There is then a section entitled 'Concept of development programme',[42] in which it is stated:

So long as developing countries depend on foreign aid, they should accept the proposition that the promotion of development

41. ibid., p. 44.   42. ibid., pp. 44–9.

55

is a joint enterprise involving the extenders and the recipients of such assistance. This partnership in the pursuit of economic growth will not bear fruit if suppliers of aid are guided more by objectives other than development, and if aid recipients are hypersensitive about suggestions originating outside their national boundaries. Assuming that there is a meaningful consensus about goals and that the partners adopt a pragmatic professional approach, agreement on the scope and character of a development plan should be possible. Periodic consultations between the Agency and members would not be confined to the subject of export forecasts; rather the consultations would be the forum in which agreement would be reached on the major assumptions underlying development programmes, including the policy measures needed to implement them. This would help ensure that the aid resources from developed countries would be put to effective use. It is also necessary to maximise the mobilisation of domestic resources for development, especially in raising the level of public savings for investment.[43]

After a discussion of the merits of development plans, the Report says: 'To summarize, the Scheme is concerned with assuring the implementation of development programmes which are feasible and operational and embody a set of policies acceptable to developing member countries as well as the international community.'[44] It is acknowledged that there will be much variation in the comprehensiveness of plans, and therefore that

Much would depend on the knowledge which the Agency possessed of the country concerned and its determination to ensure that the resources entrusted to it were used for the stated purposes. Experience[45] indicates that economic performance in relation to development can be judged correctly even when precision is technically impossible.

43. ibid., pp. 46–7.   44. ibid., p. 48.
45. Presumably the Bank's own lending experience.

Other published indications of the World Bank's attitude to leverage are to be found in the Account of Proceedings of the ODI's Conference on Effective Aid. For example:

The general point that providing aid necessarily involved intervention was accepted by most people [at the conference]. The further implication, that donor countries had a responsibility to ensure that the intervention was positive and not negative, was supported in particular by the representative of the World Bank. The World Bank had been trying to obtain greater commitment to policies favourable to development in recipient countries for some time. Complaints of 'infringement of sovereignty' had in the past been heard much earlier in the process. Although at first the Bank's intervention might have been painful, it was becoming more and more welcome. Finance Ministers sometimes incorporated agreements with the Bank on policy measures in their budget speeches. It was important to realize how far the process had already gone.[46]

In spite of this optimistic view, the Bank's general policy has been, at least until recently, to avoid public reference to, or discussion of, such issues. In fact it was stated in 1967 that the Bank's staff, unlike the Fund's, did not 'inform its Board of Governors, or anybody else' of the efforts it was making to improve, in its eyes, the general economic performance of its members. This was partly because its activities in this field were and are still, as has been said, tentative, partly because of the Fund's unhappy experiences of adverse publicity, and partly because the Bank staff felt, no doubt rightly from their point of view, that the Bank's

46. See *Effective Aid*, ODI, 1966, p. 34. In addition, in his paper on the Coordination of Aid, Mr Michael Hoffman of the World Bank states, for instance, 'It is my contention, and it is the view of the World Bank based on its experience to date, that improving the effectiveness of aid is a distinct, identifiable, and significant function or field of endeavour quite apart from the question of the amount of aid ...' (ibid., p. 67).

diplomacy was more likely to be effective if it was conducted in secrecy, with usually only a few high government officials, hopefully sympathetic to the Bank's point of view, involved in the negotiations. At any rate published references to, and accounts of, the Bank's activities in this field are meagre, and most of them do not begin to demonstrate the extent of the Bank's involvement. An exception is the Bank's publication, in September 1968, of a pamphlet, *Some Aspects of the Economic Philosophy of the World Bank*,[47] which may represent a decision to make the Bank's activities in this field more widely known. It is at any rate clearly a carefully edited and presented version of the Bank's thinking, if not of its practice, on the subject of 'leverage'. The paper by Andrew M. Kamarck on 'Appraisal of Country Economic Performance',[48] contains for example the following passages:

One of the principal lessons that the World Bank Group has learned from 20 years of experience is that the economic development or growth of a country depends primarily on a continuing improvement in the effectiveness with which that country uses its economic resources. Research activities in universities apparently have led to similar conclusions. Articles by such economists as Aukrust, Denison, Domar, and Solow have pointed out that, although there are severe difficulties of measurement, an increase in the supply of capital and in labor of unchanging quality does not explain at a maximum more than one-half of the estimated growth of gross national product (GNP) in the many countries studied ...[49]

What this means is that improving 'economic performance', or action to increase effectiveness in the use of resources, has to be the central focus of development policy. Economic develop-

47. See chapter 1, note 10.
48. *Some Aspects of the Economic Philosophy of the World Bank*, World Bank, September 1968, pp. 7–19.
49. ibid., p. 7.

ment comes through making more effective use and improving the management of all resources – existing capital as well as new capital, manpower, land, and other natural resources. This does not mean that providing more capital is not important; in fact, it may be that a greater supply of capital is essential to make it possible to take the measures necessary to improve economic performance. (Kaldor and other economists maintain that new knowledge is introduced or infused into the growth process mainly through the introduction of new equipment.) The point is that concentration primarily on increasing the amount of capital as the central element in the economic growth process represents the wrong approach to achieving faster growth ...

Fundamentally, improvement of economic performance is something that can be carried out only by the government and the people of the country concerned. It cannot be imposed from abroad. But capital from the outside can be used as an incentive to the government to take action to improve the country's economic performance. Or it can help the government to overcome some of the internal pressures and to take measures that it feels are necessary but is unable to introduce without this support from abroad. The World Bank, from its inception, has had as a principal objective helping countries to improve their economic performance. Although there has been an evolution in the methods used, in the scope of the area of the economy affected, and even in emphasis, the objective has remained unchanged ...[50]

In studying a particular country, fundamentally what has to be done is to make an adequate analysis of the way in which the national economy actually functions, to identify the constraints that influence its direction and rate of development and, finally, to identify what the government can do to improve the conditions for growth either directly or through policies that stimulate the economy ...[51]

To do this work well, the development economist should know the country thoroughly. Specifically, he should start by acquiring a knowledge of its natural and human resources, its

50. ibid., pp. 7–8.   51. ibid., p. 11.

structure of production, its position in world trade and finance, its economic history. He should acquire an understanding and appreciation of the social and institutional infrastructure: the main constraints and critical preconditions to growth have to be identified. Based on this knowledge the analyst must appraise the government's development plan or if it does not exist, he must work out an implicit or explicit development strategy, or what in very rough terms might be called a long-range development plan. This must identify the short-term policies and measures that the government can take to carry out the longer-range development strategy. Finally, the government's current activities and its policy plans must be measured against what is needed for economic development. The major test of the development policy is, therefore, the assessment of the extent to which steps are actually taken as programs are launched to remove or to reduce the main constraints to growth and to create and to improve the necessary conditions and institutions for growth. (This is not to suggest that the development economist should have a rigid approach. It is important that he should be willing to re-evaluate his findings if events and new facts show that this is necessary. What is important, however, is that government actions and plans should be judged with reference to the 'development strategy' which is fully supported by the basic analysis.) ...[52]

Specific questions that need to be answered when a particular country's economic performance is being evaluated would certainly include most of the following:

a) What is happening to the growth of production and income?

b) What is the extent of the mobilization of resources for development, and is the ratio of national savings to gross national product (GNP) growing?

c) How efficiently are existing financial resources being used?

d) How compatible is the social and institutional framework with development?

52. ibid., p. 11.

e) Is there a population growth problem? If so, what does it consist of and what, if any, effort is the government making to cope with it?

f) Is development being given appropriate emphasis compared, say, with defense?

g) How successful is the country in maintaining confidence in the currency and in the future value of savings?

h) How rapidly is import capacity increasing, i.e., what is the rate of increase of export and other foreign exchange earnings?

i) How efficiently is the country economizing on expenditures for imports?

j) How well is the balance of payments and the external debt managed; for example, does the country have an effective way of keeping track of and controlling debts incurred by government entities and enterprises?

k) How internally consistent are the development and financial policies?

What may be noted is that this list does not include, specifically, a 'development plan'. A good development plan would involve all of these factors. A country that scored high on all these points would be a country that would also have a good development plan explicitly or implicitly; such a plan is an embodiment of a set of good financial and economic policies; it is not a substitute for them ...[53]

The present position, therefore, is that in all of its lending the Bank Group (a) directly attempts – by attaching conditions to its loans – to improve the use of resources in those projects or sectors or institutions where its finance is directly involved; and (b) also tries to make a basic analysis of the economic problems and prospects of a country in cooperation with the country's government. Next – based on this analysis – it must (i) ascertain, in cooperation with the government, what is holding up faster growth and what action the government is capable of taking to correct this situation, (ii) what steps the Bank Group can reasonably expect from the government toward attaining

53. ibid., p. 12.

improved economic performance, concurrently with the extension of Bank Group assistance . . .[54]

At one extreme, there are countries where the role of the Bank Group is very small. The reason for this may be that the country concerned has reached the stage where it needs very little help from abroad, or that the political or governmental situation is such that the government is relatively helpless to accomplish anything much in improving economic performance, or that most of its external capital comes from a source that is not interested in whatever conclusions the Group may reach in its economic analysis. In such cases, if anything can be done at all, the Group may have to limit itself to the influence of the basic economic analysis process or the improvement it can obtain through financing a particular sector or succession of sectors. At the other extreme are countries where the Bank Group is the predominant source of external capital and where sufficient elements in the government are both eager and capable of taking action to improve economic performance in a number of ways if they are supported by the Group in getting the government officially to agree to such measures. In these cases, the Group may agree with the country, in a more or less formal form, on a lending program in a number of sectors and on understandings of the policy actions that the government will take to improve performance in significant fields. Most countries would, of course, lie between these two extremes.

The measures to improve performance that are economically desirable and possible vary from country to country. As the focus is always on a particular country, its problems and its potential, the procedures that need to be emphasized vary from country to country, and from time to time in a particular country. The World Bank Group has to look at the entire development process; and in the course of the economic analysis, conclusions have to be reached as to which are the areas or sectors that are most important at the particular time and in which progress should and can be made. In some countries, the most important measure may be to have a more stable price level or a better

54. ibid., pp. 16–17.

monetary or fiscal policy. In these countries, the Bank Group works in parallel with the Fund, and what the Bank Group and the Fund try to accomplish may be identical or the work of one may supplement that of the other. In other countries, other measures in quite different sectors may be the strategic ones. For example, in one country in Africa the Group's analysis came to the conclusion that the most important immediate measure to be taken was to raise the price paid to the farmer for peanuts, the most important export of the country. Because the government had maintained at too low a level the price that its market board paid to the farmers, the farmers had cut down on production. The result was that the foreign exchange at the disposal of the government to be used for financing imports of equipment was too low. Here the most important item was the price of peanuts, and the Bank Group devoted its attention to that problem. In another country, the crucial improvement in policy that may be needed and feasible may well be general arrangements for the management of industry, the financing of public utilities or agriculture, etc.[55]

These quotations from Kamarck's paper do not show the extent, and in particular the rigidity, of the Bank's insistence on particular policies. But the paper does state publicly that the Bank is now deeply involved in the business of setting 'general performance conditions' on its lending. Among the Bank's staff various views are expressed on how this has come about. The process has clearly been sporadic, and has had something to do with personalities and chance circumstances. There are some within the Bank who see a general and inevitable trend, with the Bank moving steadily from an original, rather narrow banking view, towards much greater awareness of development problems in general. There are others who point to specific events and constraints. The Bank's activities in this field have, at any rate, not yet been fully systematized; there is still some internal opposition to

55. ibid., pp. 17–18.

this, and considerable divergence of views. It is therefore difficult to trace the history of Bank involvement and to explain its present operation in any coherent manner.

From early days the Bank has from time to time made general observations on countries' economic policies. For instance, in 1949 the Bank was already saying to Chile that it should make an effort to reduce inflation as a prerequisite for Bank lending. Occasionally it made specific representations; Peru for instance, in the 1950s, agreed not to accept more short-term suppliers' credits. Sometimes the Bank succeeded in persuading a government to raise the rates charged by, or to reduce the number of people employed in, railways or power companies, even when no particular Bank project was involved. On a number of occasions the Bank has ceased to make commitments to lend: for example, in Colombia, under Rojas Pinilla, from 1956 to 1958; in Brazil, under Goulart, from 1962 until the new military government took power in 1964; in Argentina, under Illia and in the first few months of the new military government, until this government appointed Dr Krieger Vasena as Finance Minister; in Guatemala, in the early sixties, over the issue of Guatemala's sterling debt; in Bolivia, for a period after the 1952 revolution; and in Cuba.

In addition, apart from occasions when there was a question of the Bank ceasing to lend, the Bank also became more willing to offer its advice and expertise in matters not directly connected with specific projects. In the 1950s efforts were made to build up national planning offices in Colombia, Peru and Chile. An agricultural mission was sent to Uruguay in 1950 and to Chile in 1951. The Bank's involvement in Colombia has been long and fairly continuous. In 1956, the Bank set up its Economic Development Institute (EDI) mainly to provide courses on general problems, although the emphasis has now shifted to teaching methods of project evaluation.

More important perhaps, the Bank began to produce general reports on countries' economic situation. Originally, Bank reports, rather like IMF reports, had a formal purpose. IMF reports conclude formally by recommending to the Directors that a country be permitted to retain certain exchange restrictions. Bank reports were exercises to determine a country's creditworthiness; they concluded, and still usually conclude, by saying that the Bank and other potential lenders would be justified in lending to the country concerned, and they generally make some estimate of the amount of lending that is needed and justified. From this rather narrow concentration on creditworthiness, the reports developed into general analyses of countries' economies. During the 1950s the Bank produced some big reports on a number of countries, resulting from what were called General Survey Missions, which were intended to contribute to the formulation of national investment programmes and were published by the Johns Hopkins Press. These reports are of quite a different nature from subsequent reports, and in general cover a wider field; they were also written with the help, or under the direction, of consultants from outside the Bank. Current Bank reports are not intended for publication, but more as guides for Bank policy; their circulation is restricted to the government of the country concerned, the Board and a few privileged individuals. Most of them now usually cover not simply the country's borrowing capacity and needs, but, for instance, its fiscal and monetary policies, investment policy, the balance of payments, prices and wages, the treatment of the private sector, and sometimes also agricultural and educational policies; they usually contain forecasts for the future, especially of the balance of payments and debt-servicing capacity, and full statistical tables. The Bank fairly regularly produces reports 'in depth' for countries for which it organizes consortia and consultative groups, and for certain major countries which are large borrowers from the Bank, like Brazil. For other countries the reports are usually shorter, although the size of Bank reports is not closely related to the size of the countries reported on: there was recently a very large report on Guyana, in which it was presumably considered important[56] that the government's economic policies should be successful. The Bank's aim is to send missions of varying sizes and at varying intervals of time to all the countries to which it lends.

Another very important development in the Bank's activities has been the setting up of consortia and consultative groups presided over by the Bank.[57] The first consortium, the India consortium set up in 1958, arose as an *ad hoc* response to India's critical foreign exchange situation, and subsequently developed a concern with India's general development problems. The Pakistan consortium had its origin largely in Pakistan's desire to be treated like India. The subsequent consultative groups were more consciously designed to mark the Bank's, and it was hoped other lenders', interest in the development of the countries for which the groups were set up. In Latin America groups were set up for Colombia and Peru, and contemplated, from time to time, for Chile and Brazil. The Bank, in agreeing to operate a consultative group for a particular country, demonstrated its general approval of the policies of the country, tried to ensure that the lending policies of

56. After the CIA's part in installing the government of Forbes Burnham.

57. See John White, *Pledged to Development*, ODI, 1967, for a full history and analysis of these mechanisms. See also the Bank's *Annual Reports*, which state the official purposes of the mechanisms.

other countries and agencies were conducive to their success, provided documentation for the group, and in general offered to act as the country's special adviser.

Partly as a result of these developments, and also, perhaps, contributing to their momentum, the Economics Department of the Bank was in 1965 reorganized and reinforced by a considerable influx of economists. Another reason for expanding the Economics Department was to strengthen the position of the Area Departments in relation to that of the Projects Department, by giving the Area Departments a more central position in the structure of the Bank; the Projects Department was, and to some extent remains, the 'core' of the Bank, as a Bank official expressed it. In general the Bank's Area Departments are responsible for the selection and development of projects in their areas and for country appraisals and missions;[58] the Projects Department for accepting or rejecting projects submitted to it by Area Departments on the basis of a technical evaluation of their viability; and the Economics Department for producing functional reports and more specialized economic and econometric analyses. The Economics Department is now also very much engaged in attempting to define criteria for 'good performance' and it also sometimes provides personnel for missions to the recipient countries, and to service consultative groups. The Bank's staff has in the last few years doubled in size, and there are complaints of inefficiency, slowness, and of increasing rigidity in procedures. Private businesses complain of the Bank's 'civil service mentality' and unwillingness to make rapid decisions. In addition, there are criticisms of the narrow range of competence and national origins of the Bank's staff; especially at high levels, Bank officials are overwhelmingly

58. In 1967 the Bank had four Area Departments, one of which was responsible for the Western Hemisphere.

bankers and economists from North America and Northern Europe.[59]

In the past few years rather more deliberate and systematic attempts have been made to influence the policies of borrowing countries. In principle, the Bank expects to come to some sort of agreement on present and future policies with the countries in which it is likely to finance projects, and to have a continuing discussion of and interest in these policies. In a country whose economic problems are particularly acute in the Bank's view, the Bank sometimes asks for a formal Memorandum of Understanding on specific issues, similar to the I M F's Letters of Intent. The question of the country's general performance does not necessarily arise specifically in connection with negotiations for project loans and the Bank would be most unlikely to stop disbursement of a loan once the agreement had been signed. But, in theory, the Bank now makes its decisions as loans arise partly on the basis of its view of the country's general performance. It will not discuss a lending programme unless it is satisfied with the country's general policies. A very good project, it is said, may be rejected on the grounds that the country's general policies are 'not conducive to economic development and investment'.

59. It is possible that the Bank's new President, Mr McNamara, will change this situation, although the staff is likely to be even larger. In his speech to the Board of Governors on 30 September 1968, McNamara said: 'With the doubling of Bank Group lending and with the increase in the complexity of our operations, there will clearly be a need for an increase in the total professional staff of the Bank, as well as for some streamlining of our procedures. We are now engaged in a world-wide recruiting drive to find people with the high standards and dedication that have always been the attribute of its staff. I am anxious that this should really be an International Bank, in fact as well as in name, and I intend to ensure that we move steadily in the direction of the widest possible distribution in the nationalities of our staff.'

This view of things was embodied in formal procedural changes made within the Bank in 1965. An Economic Committee was then set up, parallel to the already existing Loan Committee. Loans, to be agreed by the Bank staff before they go to the Board, must now be accepted first by the Economic Committee, which has before it memoranda defining policy issues from the Area Departments, and makes recommendations on the acceptance or rejection of the proposal for a loan on the basis of its view of the general economic performance of the country concerned. It also reviews the Bank's economic reports and studies, with the purpose of ensuring greater uniformity and compatibility between them.[60] The function of the Loan Committee is to determine whether or not the particular project is satisfactory. Loans must therefore be approved by both Committees before they are finally accepted.

The effective application of these ideas and procedures depends on the degree of the Bank's involvement in particular countries, and on the personalities concerned. The ideas, for the moment at any rate, are more accepted in the Western Hemisphere Department than elsewhere in the Bank, with the possible exception of those concerned with

60. But see this chapter, note 66. On the Economic Committee, see also Andrew M. Kamarck, article cited this chapter, note 48, who says: 'In the last few years, there has been a further major evolution in Bank policy in that consistent and deliberate analysis of country economic performance has been made a major objective of the Bank Group's economic work. The earlier Staff Economic Committee, which tended to focus on questions of creditworthiness, has been replaced by an Economic Committee chaired by the Economic Adviser to the President. The main focus of this Committee has been on evaluation of economic performance and the formation of Bank policy to secure better economic performance, as well as on what should be the appropriate set of loan terms for the country. In this process, staff members of the International Monetary Fund also participate and contribute their experience and expertise.'

the South Asian subcontinent. In countries where there is no particular history of World Bank concern with general policies, the scrutiny of the Economic Committee may be more formal than real.[61]

An important question is whether the Bank has any intention of trying actively to change the policies of the countries to which it might lend. In a country with which the Bank's relations are distant, the Bank may simply decide to lend or not to lend and that will be that. The decision may be an inducement to this country, or others, to adopt policies of which the Bank is likely to approve. But elsewhere the Bank may actually become engaged in negotiations with the country, aimed at improving its policies in

61. The arrival of McNamara has given new impetus to these ideas. This is particularly clear in the case of Indonesia, but there are signs of increasing Bank interest in general policies in other countries as well. For example, in an interview published in the *Banker*, March 1969, McNamara said: 'In the Fall of 1968, the Bank posted a resident mission to Indonesia with responsibilities for advising the Indonesian authorities on questions of economic policy and administration; on the effective use of technical assistance, including studies to identify and prepare projects, the selection of consultants, the framing of terms of reference; and on related matters. This is the first time that the World Bank Group has become deeply involved in the initiative for development planning and with implementation by a member country. If the need arises we will not hesitate to take on similar responsibilities in other countries.' In the same interview McNamara was asked what he meant when he said that the plans for expanded lending in Africa depended on 'effective collaboration' from African countries, and he answered: 'What I meant was that the African countries must create the atmosphere that is conducive to development. This would include: (a) A willingness to make the hard decisions necessary to assuring a sound and feasible programme for development. This could include tax measures, and decisions concerning the direction of development and the choice of projects that might be politically unpopular; (b) A willingness to accept and implement advice from outside experts – World Bank or others – as to sectoral and project priorities.'

the eyes of the Bank. Ideally, in the Bank's view, such negotiations would enable as many countries as possible to
become suitable borrowers from the Bank and as few as
possible to be relegated to the Bank's 'black list'.

The Bank's methods of negotiating are not always conducive to this objective. In theory, the idea is that the Bank
should achieve improvements in borrowing countries'
policies by discussion and 'dialogue', by a process of give
and take, from which the objectively 'best' solution will
finally emerge. Such a process of dialogue no doubt sometimes occurs, within the limits set by what is acceptable to
the Bank (see below). But frequently the Bank gives the
impression of having made up its own mind on the issues,
sometimes with little prior discussion with the government
concerned, and then of being merely determined to persuade
the government to adopt its solutions.[62] This process itself
can be more or less flexibly conducted. The Bank certainly
has a reputation for dogmatism and for laying down specific
conditions, on whose acceptance or non-acceptance the
Bank's lending decisions will depend, without trying to
ensure that the government understands and sympathizes
with their purpose. A further claim is made by Bank officials
that it is not a question of 'imposing' policies, but of
'finding the right people to support'; this claim is somewhat
disingenuous, for the purpose of this exercise can only be to
make it easier for the 'right people' (and the Bank) to
impose their views on other members of the government and
other sectors of the population.[63]

62. An indication that this is so is provided in Andrew M. Kamarck's
paper cited this chapter, note 48. See quotation, pp. 59–60, especially the
phrase: '... the analyst must appraise the government's development
plan or if it does not exist, he must work out an *implicit* or explicit
development strategy ...' (my italics).

63. See also Andrew M. Kamarck, ibid., p. 17, in which he says:

The role of Bank reports, like the application of Bank ideas on involvement, has not been systematized and varies from country to country and from mission to mission. Some reports are more operational than others, in the sense that they are intended to provide the criteria on which the Bank's view of the country's performance will be based. Such reports generally go through a number of drafts. The first draft, which is usually only seen by the government concerned, may contain some strong criticisms of the government's policies and some proposals for changes. The aim is then that it should be possible to eliminate the grounds for criticism through negotiating changes in policies. If such negotiations are unsuccessful, the report may never get to the stage when it is seen by the Directors and receives even the limited circulation described above. It is said that this is partly because the Bank prefers not to present very negative reports to potential lenders. The result is that only the government of the country concerned and the staff of the Bank officially see the report and know of the specific recommendations made by the Bank. Other reports are fairly general and innocuous from the start. The information, opinions and projections they contain will then, to a greater or lesser extent, and depending on whether the government bothers to read them,[64] presumably contribute to the formulation of policy. Reports for countries for

---

'What is attempted is to give support to policies and actions that are conducive to growth; it is *not* to buy, with loans or credits, policies the Bank Group likes. The difference may appear subtle but it is enormously important. In the latter case, it would mean getting a policy decision that the executing government in reality did not believe in. What is sought instead is to give support to those elements and those policies that are helping growth and through the support strengthen them and thus encourage a more rapid rate of growth.'

64. And which members of the government can read English, since they are not translated and are always written in English.

which there are, or were, operating consultative groups may be specifically intended to guide the policies of other lenders as well as those of the country concerned; all Bank reports, in so far as they are made available, may of course serve this purpose.[65]

Bank reports, while they sometimes provide the most comprehensive analysis available of a country's economic situation and prospects, have been criticized as well as praised. Inside the Bank, the concern is usually that the purposes of particular reports and missions and the effect they are intended to have on policies have not been made sufficiently clear. The decisions rest largely with the head of the Bank's mission. Among the few outsiders who have seen Bank reports there are also criticisms of the standards of economic analysis in them, of the lack of critical evaluation of official statistics provided by the government concerned and reproduced in the reports, and of the existence of inconsistencies between reports.[66] A general feature of Bank reports is that they very rarely make clear the assumptions on which their economic projections and proposals are based, and the effects of their assumptions on a number of issues; nor do they suggest alternative ends, or even alternative means of achieving the recommended ends, when they

65. On Bank reports, see also John White, *Pledged to Development*, ODI, 1967, p. 72.

66. For example, the policies for increasing agricultural production proposed to the Guyana government depended on the assumption of a negative response by producers to a higher price for rice; in other reports, much emphasis is put on increasing agricultural prices in order to stimulate production. There appear also to be inconsistencies in the field of primary commodities, both in the sense of inconsistent forecasts on future prices and markets, and in the sense that, for example, Bank economists in Africa are recommending the introduction of palm oil and thus threatening the position of long-established producers of this commodity in Malaya and the prices of palm oil in general.

propose a set of policies for implementation by the government concerned.[67]

Why has this greater Bank involvement in the general policies of developing countries come about?

There are two main explanations current in the Bank, as well as a number of subsidiary ones. One is that the Bank's concern arose primarily because of the increasingly heavy indebtedness of its member countries, a problem which directly concerned the Bank as a big international lender and which made it necessary to ensure that recipient countries would be in a position to repay debts in the future. The second is that the Bank, like other international institutions, inevitably came to concentrate increasingly on the problem of economic development in its member countries. It had to take more account of their need to develop and therefore began to try to find solutions to development problems and, in some cases, to persuade countries to adopt these solutions. Some people in the Bank have categorically affirmed that one explanation was correct and the other false, and *vice versa*.[68] There are

67. See chapter 4.

68. Andrew M. Kamarck's paper (cited this chapter, note 48) contains versions of both these explanations; on pp. 9 and 10 he says: 'In international lending to governments prior to the organization of the World Bank, little attention was paid to the particular use that the borrower would make of the funds received. Defaults on international loans were widespread in the 1930s, and it was concluded that a principal reason for the defaults was improper use of the funds by the borrowers. Consequently, when the World Bank Charter was being written, a provision that Bank lending should be for projects was included. Essentially, this meant that the Bank should lend only for clearly defined and agreed purposes which would result in an increase in the productive capacity of the borrowing country, and that appropriate institutional arrangements in that country should exist or should be created to ensure that the purposes of the loan would be achieved.

'From the beginning, the Bank has used this technique of lending

certainly several examples of the Bank becoming involved in the general economic policies of a country as a direct result of its debt problems. India is perhaps the most notable example; more recently, Ghana and Indonesia received Bank attention after major debt-rescheduling

---

as a means of securing some progress in a more effective use of resources, both borrowed and domestic, in the recipient country.... Over the years, therefore, even when the Bank made only a relatively small contribution to international capital flows, it made a significant contribution toward improving the management of resources in at least those parts of the economies that it was directly aiding.'

And on p. 15 he says: 'Along with this growth of the greater responsibility of the World Bank Group in development finance, there has been growth in the sentiment for more positive action to obtain better country economic performance. In part, this has stemmed from the economic research in the universities, which was mentioned earlier, and in part from a feeling of disappointment in the progress made thus far by the less-developed countries and, consequently, from the desire to modify the way in which economic aid has been given.

'A very important force in this evolution was the creation of the International Development Association (IDA) in 1960 to make capital available on soft terms – i.e., with a very large grant equivalent – to the poorer developing countries. As long as there was only the World Bank proper, it was easy to overlook the fact that Bank loans included a subsidy element (with the credit of the richer countries behind the Bank, the Bank was able to borrow and to lend at rates generally below what the developing countries would otherwise have had to pay). It was easy to be influenced by the feeling that the Bank was a bank, to overlook the Bank's practice of securing better performance in the projects and sectors financed, and to conclude that the economic performance of the borrower's economy was outside of the Bank's interest. With the creation of IDA and the provision by IDA of credits which, at present terms, are equivalent to a grant element of more than 80 per cent of the face value of the credit (calculated at a discount rate of 10 per cent), it becomes obvious that what is involved is something quite different from normal investment banking – that, in fact, the World Bank Group is engaged in development finance and inescapably must be concerned with the performance of the economy as a whole.'

operations; and when Colombia in 1955 wanted to contract new debt from French suppliers, the Bank, concerned about the level of public debt, decided to review the purposes of the debt and studied Colombia's public investment programme.[69] On the other hand in recent years there has been increasing concern about the 'effectiveness' of aid, especially in Washington, and aid theorists and practitioners have increasingly been talking about the principles of 'self help', 'aid leverage', and 'performance criteria'. People in the United States AID, and some in the Bank, were arguing that physical investment alone would not make an effective contribution to development if the country's policies were 'wrong'. Capital inflows might help, but more was to be expected from technical assistance and the 'discipline' that came with the capital inflows. It was necessary to support people in the government who were trying to do the 'right' thing; when the country's policies 'went astray', lending agencies could be most useful by saying they would stop lending until policies changed. It was natural that the Bank, as a leading development institution, should come to play a leading role in this new school of thought.

Probably both these phenomena have contributed to the Bank's evolution. There are other explanations and contributory causes, interlinked no doubt. Partly because of countries' indebtedness, it became more important for the Bank to feel that at least its own projects were priority projects; this meant that it was necessary to try to see the projects as part of a total investment programme. The Western Hemisphere Department was, in many ways, the Area Department most concerned with relating projects to

69. As early as 1949–50, the Bank stated in its *Annual Report* that it must 'ensure that the maintenance of service on Bank loans is not jeopardised by the emergence of conditions which might reasonably be prevented.'

general economic policies. Its advance over other departments in this respect can probably be explained mainly by the fact that it was dealing with countries which were semi-industrialized, whose incomes per head were generally higher than in Africa and Asia, and whose economies were generally more complex. In particular, Latin-American countries have on the whole been the first developing countries to experience in an acute form the problems of inflation, heavy debt and balance of payments crises. Finally, the United States is more closely concerned in Latin America and the Bank itself has been involved in Latin America for longer than elsewhere.

More recently, the Bank has had to be concerned with making a case for the replenishment of IDA. There is a feeling, especially in Washington, that the way to persuade the rich countries to provide more money is to demonstrate not simply that the money itself is being 'well spent', but that developing countries are making what can be described as satisfactory efforts of their own. Hence the Bank's exercise to demonstrate the amount of additional resources developing countries could 'effectively' absorb; and hence also, in part, the efforts to persuade Latin-American countries in particular to adopt 'sensible' policies. In addition, there are those who see, with or without alarm, the greater efforts to persuade developing countries to 'help themselves' as a substitute for willingness to increase the level of financial resources provided by the rich countries. Others point to the coincidence of the Bank's change of direction with the presidency of Mr Woods; others to its coincidence with the enlargement of the Economics Department (which may have been partly effect and partly cause).

At any rate the change is certainly taking place to a much greater extent than is generally supposed. Those who oppose it within the Bank do so mainly on the grounds that the Bank is being over-ambitious, is diverging too far from its original purposes as expressed in its statutes, and is unlikely, in any case, to be effective in changing policies. The Bank's ability to exercise pressure is mainly based on its ability to provide financial resources. But, of the three institutions primarily involved in the business of pressure, the World Bank's traditional method of providing finance is the least well adapted for use as a 'lever'. The Bank cannot, or at least does not, link the actual disbursement of its project loans directly to the observance of its conditions on general performance. It can only delay commitment. Usually it must negotiate separately on the two issues. Project loans arise at irregular intervals, although Bank missions visit countries with relative regularity. It may happen that the Bank would particularly like to have an effect on policy at a time when there is no project loan pending. In any case, the Bank's financial contribution to projects is not usually of sufficient importance in particular instances for the government to be willing to change policies in order to get it, especially as the Projects Department in the Bank can have its powerfully negative effect whatever the views of the Area Departments on the virtue of supporting a government's programme. Insistence on general 'performance conditions' may not mean better performance; it may just mean no Bank projects. There are therefore some in the Bank who would like to be able to make programme loans on a much larger scale, and the question whether or not the Bank should make such loans is currently being discussed.[70] There are others who say that

70. See, for instance, Kamarck (cited this chapter, note 48), p. 18: 'The most effective way to extend external finance in relation to the particular improvements in policies and actions that are supported is still far from being fully understood. A few principles appear to be

the Bank is a bank and should stick to what it is good at, i.e. projects.

Recently the Bank has been adding, consciously or unconsciously, to its armoury. In countries in which it is heavily involved and which have a need for external finance, the Bank is likely to consider setting up consultative groups. The offer to do this can in theory be an inducement to come to an agreement with the Bank, although in practice, in Latin America at least, the Bank has not found notable enthusiasm for consultative groups. In the countries for which there already are or have been consultative groups[71] the Bank can and does delay calling a meeting of the group until it is satisfied with the country's policies. In a less formal sense also the Bank's approval or disapproval of a country may have some effect on the policies of other lenders, as in the case of the IMF. A direction in which the Bank might move is that of becoming the coordinator, even the controller, of other forms of external finance. Already in Latin America there are signs of a united front between lending agencies, at least as far as the three main ones are concerned; the World Bank of course is not always dominant, but in some countries it is. The World Bank has also

emerging from experience, however. For example, financing a road project can often help secure some needed improvements in policies affecting the whole highway sector as well as in policies affecting the whole economy. But, financing a *road* project can rarely help secure improvements in policies affecting the *electric power* sector. Basically, for improvements to be made, there has to be some direct identification on the part of the agency concerned with the financing being received. The impact on general policies comes from the identification of the interests of the Ministry of Finance, Central Bank, and Ministry of Economy or Planning Board with increasing the import of external resources. As the Bank Group has not made any program loans, it has not had any experience with the radius of effectiveness of this type of external finance.' For a definition of programme loans, see pp. 91–2.

71. Peru and Colombia.

been known to try to persuade the Inter-American Bank either to stop lending to a country, or at least to push for policy changes which the World Bank thinks necessary; these efforts have so far met with partial success. On one occasion the Bank 'told' the New York commercial banks to stop lending to a country – with success.[72] The ability of Latin-American countries to choose between lenders with different policies is decreasing somewhat, and their need to agree with one institution correspondingly increasing.

The proposal for Supplementary Financial Measures,[73] if it had been accepted in the form in which the Bank made it and if the Bank had acted as the managing agency, would have increased the Bank's ability to influence policies. By how much is uncertain: as was said in the Bank, 'the Bank is doing it anyway' and does not feel that the size of the funds contemplated for Supplementary Finance would have enabled the scheme to make a significant difference to the Bank's ability to exercise leverage. In any case, the scheme emerged from UNCTAD II more dead than alive.

Finally, it is arguable that the considerable prestige of the World Bank does have some effect on its own. World Bank reports are quite widely, if wrongly, taken as an authoritative and impartial view, free from political *arrière pensées*. The Bank certainly has fewer hesitations than some other institutions about making criticisms of its member countries and is relatively free from political inhibitions of this variety. The World Bank, it is often said, is a 'lenders' organization', whereas the Inter-American Development Bank, for instance, is a 'borrowers' organization' and therefore less prepared to be 'tough'. Some of the Bank's appraisals carry considerable weight and may even contain revelations which, if leaked, can create internal political

72. See chapter 3, section on Colombia.
73. See pp. 54–6.

difficulties for the government concerned.[74] Moreover the governments of developing countries may believe that they should pay attention to observations made in Bank reports in order to get Bank finance, even when the observations are in fact made rather casually and are not intended to give rise to conditions on Bank lending. This is especially true because the drafts of mission reports are given to governments before they have been discussed in the Bank itself. In addition, the Bank, by its determination to collect figures, has probably had some useful effect on the quality of statistical information. It may, by its probings and pressure, have contributed to a greater preoccupation with economic necessities, although the Bank has also been criticized for publishing excessive quantities of 'meaningless' statistics, quoting them uncritically and thus perpetuating a damaging faith in their validity. Certainly Bank views should, and sometimes do, give rise to discussion and reappraisals of policy.[75]

There was also a view in the Bank, now endorsed by Mr McNamara,[76] that the Bank's capacity to influence policies might be greater if it had permanent representation in developing countries. The Bank has, from time to time, had representatives in Latin-American countries. By 1967 they had all been withdrawn, or at least the Bank officials who were still resident in Latin America were not referred to as 'representatives'. The official Bank view was that, in the age of jet aeroplanes, it was simpler to fly people to Latin America whenever this was felt to be necessary and to

74. For example in Costa Rica, the Bank's criticisms of educational policy reached the press, made front page news and gave rise to quite violent debate in parliament.

75. The process of course ought to be mutual.

76. See his Address to the Board of Governors, Washington, 30 September, 1968.

centralize administration and policy-making in Washington. It was felt also that Bank officials, if they were resident in developing countries, might be in danger of losing their (Washington) sense of perspective. Bank officials do visit Latin-American countries frequently and know their economies well. But it may be that if, like AID officials, they are more exposed to opinions in the countries they are dealing with, the possibility of discussion and give-and-take on policies will be somewhat greater.

Apart from these questions about the suitability or the capability of the Bank as an institution to have an influence on general economic policies, a few doubts are also occasionally expressed at high levels in the Bank about the directions in which the Bank's influence is exercised. These doubts are sometimes based on the feeling that the Bank does not necessarily know what is right for particular countries; its function should, at most, be to point to possible difficulties and possible solutions and the Bank should avoid arrogance and dogmatism in its dealings with governments. On the whole, however, there is considerable conviction that the Bank knows what needs to be done; the question asked is usually how to persuade governments to do it.

There also exist doubts about the fact that, as one official put it, the Bank's agreements with some countries, especially those in Latin America, tend to look like 'carbon copies' of Fund agreements. The Bank is certainly entering the IMF's field. This is justified, within the Bank, by the contention that in Latin America the most urgent problems are those with which the IMF has for some time been dealing. Short-term problems, it is said, are so difficult to solve that preoccupation with them is unavoidable; the problem of inflation is 'overwhelming'; the Bank must be involved if only because of the increasingly acute problems of indebtedness. Quite apart from whether or not this is so, there is of course an argument for leaving these matters to the Fund. On the other hand it can be argued that the Fund and the Bank, from their different points of view – the one of monetary stability, the other of investment policy – have necessarily converged; that there is a group of questions, mainly fiscal, which affect the operations of both institutions; and that there are connected questions with which one is clearly more concerned than the other. According to this theory, the Bank would give way to the Fund on exchange rates[77] and the Fund would give way to the Bank on investment policy, even if this affected stability.[78] Both institutions have views on the causes of inflation, but the Bank's views are largely derived from discussions with the Fund; in fact the Bank usually either obtains fiscal and monetary sections of its reports on particular countries from the Fund, or invites the Fund's opinion on its own drafts. It is certainly recognized that co-operation is necessary in order to 'avoid duplication' and conflicting advice; it is claimed that co-operation between the Bank and the Fund is fairly well organized and Fund officials attend meetings of the Bank's Economic Committee. Possibly the best justification for the Bank's concern with Fund policies would be that the Bank wanted to ensure that the Fund's short-term exigencies did not conflict with the Bank's long-term concerns. However, 'long-term' is for the Bank a relative concept and not very different from 'short term'; for the moment, the Bank either does not question Fund policies, or is just as likely to

77. But the Bank has been deeply concerned in questions of devaluation; see for example chapter 3, section on Colombia. The Bank has also claimed devaluation in India as one clear case in which its leverage was effective.

78. But there is little evidence of the Bank pressing for expansion, and some contrary evidence. See, for example, this chapter, note 6.

be more exigent than the Fund on deflationary policies as it is, for example, to argue the case for expansion.

There are some in the Bank who would like it to exercise influence in different directions. One specific suggestion was that it should concentrate on what is sometimes called 'institution building': on building up and strengthening the mechanism for taking economic decisions in developing countries, so that they can manage their economies more efficiently, know what is happening and choose rationally. This suggestion was based on the feeling that at the time in some countries people tended to think of the business of project selection, economic forecasting, collecting statistics, and so on, as 'religious rites' which the Bank went through; the people watched; they were not themselves of the priesthood.[79] In this view the Bank should be less concerned with problem-solving, more with encouraging others to solve problems.

A few would like the Bank to be more 'adventurous', more concerned, for instance, with social problems. This is a view not at all widespread at high levels in the Bank. When it is held, it is sometimes qualified by the observation that the Bank's freedom of action is limited by the need to maintain its reputation in conservative financial circles. The Bank jealously guards the reputation which it feels that it has for cautiousness, soundness and reliability. It certainly has less of a reputation than other international institutions for 'wasting' its funds and has achieved a remarkable amount of respect in the international financial community,[80]

79. In Peru feasibility studies are 'los informes de los gringos', 'el trabajo de los técnicos'.

80. Scammel wrote in *International Monetary Policy*, second edition, Macmillan, 1961: 'A notable feature of the Bank is that it has gained the respect and confidence of business and financial interests, being itself run as a business by bankers in close collaboration with Wall Street and financial interests throughout the world.'

although it has also been criticized even there for excessive cautiousness. It might lose some of this respect if it was 'adventurous' in the projects it financed or in the policies it promoted. It is not so clear that it would lose, as is also argued, its ability to raise funds in private capital markets, or its triple-A rating on Wall Street. These things depend more on the size of the Bank's government backing than on the soundness of its projects, which is one of the reasons why some bankers and businessmen feel that the Bank is unnecessarily cautious. The Bank's uncalled subscriptions are equal to nearly seven times its outstanding debt.[81] Its bond issues have often been over-subscribed, and are regarded as exceptionally safe investments. The Bank's main difficulty in raising funds is in getting permission from governments for access to their markets. It is therefore with governments that the Bank must be mainly concerned. For the replenishment of IDA the Bank of course depends wholly on governments. Governments are likely to make their decisions on the basis of their general attitude towards developing countries, and on the basis of the state of their capital markets, as well as on the basis of the policies of the World Bank. Moreover their attitude on the latter might be expected, in many cases, to be more 'progressive' than that of the international financial community or of the Bank staff itself.

There is also the question of the autonomy of the Bank staff. There is no doubt that the staff has considerable freedom to make its own decisions, and that, unlike in the

81. The Bank has thus been very much more cautious than its Articles of Agreement stipulate; Article III, section 3 says that 'the total amount outstanding of guarantees, participations in loans and direct loans made by the Bank' must not exceed 'one hundred percent of the unimpaired subscribed capital, reserves and surplus of the Bank'. Mr McNamara's decision to double Bank lending will have some effect on this situation.

IMF, a great deal is done without the Directors being consulted or even informed. It is possible that, although many *governments* might be more inclined towards 'progressive' policies than the Bank staff, the same is not true of the Bank's Directors, most of whom are central bankers or Finance Ministry officials primarily interested in the IMF.[82] But this ought not to be a factor of any fundamental importance. What is more important is that the Bank staff's autonomy is not questioned partly because it acts within a framework of which the major countries approve. But Bank officials seem either to have a mistaken view of the distance it would be possible to move without going outside this framework, or merely to be doing what they are anyway inclined to do, whether they use the framework as an excuse or not.

Although the Bank probably has not reached the limits it would be possible for it to go to, such limits clearly exist. The Bank could not be more 'progressive' than the United States government. Examples of United States intervention in the decisions of the Bank already exist.[83] If the Bank began to support policies in developing countries which the United States government, or other influential governments, considered incompatible with their interests, such intervention would become more frequent. If the intervention was ignored, the Bank could be prevented from raising funds in major capital markets and the IDA would not be replenished.

Nevertheless, for the moment the Bank's orientation appears to be determined as much by the inclinations of its

82. Although they may have deputies with interests in development.
83. The best-known and clearest example of the Bank yielding to political pressure is in the decision not to finance the Aswan dam in Egypt, when the United States and Britain began to quarrel with Egypt in 1955–6.

staff as by the sources of its finance. It is also to some extent determined simply by the fact that the Bank is a bank. If it is to continue to operate profitably, it must be concerned with financial stability, legality and the orderly settlement of debts. Finally, the Bank, presumably for all these reasons, has remained faithful to its statutes in its concern to 'promote foreign private investment' and to ensure that 'due regard' is paid to 'business conditions in its members' territories'.[84] Such considerations set limits on the range of policies advocated by the Bank. They exclude for example any toleration, let alone advocacy, of revolution.

THE UNITED STATES AGENCY FOR INTERNATIONAL DEVELOPMENT

Of the three institutions, the AID has most clearly and publicly formulated its theories on influencing the general economic policies of developing countries, or 'leverage'. The AID's relative lack of inhibition can be explained by its need to convince Congress of the usefulness of aid, and by the fact that it has been decided that one of the best ways of doing this is to show to Congress that the AID is effective in influencing the general economic policies of developing countries.

AID documents state that aid is an instrument of United States foreign policy, and that as such it is best suited to the promotion of economic development.[85] The AID's publication, *Principles of Foreign Economic Assistance*, states that three principles govern the allocation of United States aid:

84. See Articles of Agreement, Article 1.
85. See quotation from the AID's *Program Guidance Manual*, chapter 1, note 4.

(1) the effectiveness with which the country can use available resources – both internal and external – to promote the economic growth of the country;

(2) the importance to the United States of sustaining or accelerating the economic growth of the country;

(3) the availability to the country of other external resources in a suitable form.[86]

This document continues:

Aid is most effective in bringing about the transition from dependence or stagnation to self-sustaining growth if it is concentrated on the countries that are doing most to help themselves. There it serves as a catalytic agent which permits the mobilisation of a much larger development effort. Self-help is therefore the dominant theme of our major assistance efforts.[87]

The AID also publishes a number of discussion papers written by members of its staff. One of these describes AID methods of influencing policies through aid and states for example:

AID has increasingly recognized that economic aid can promote development not simply by supplementing the host country's limited capital and technical resources but also by exerting influence on host country policies and programmes. As we have become more aware of aid's potential leverage role, we have experimented with techniques for exercising such leverage more effectively.[88]

86. *Principles of Foreign Economic Assistance*, Agency for International Development, Washington, 1963, p. 3.

87. ibid., p. 4. See also the AID's annual submissions to Congress, *Proposed Mutual Defense and Development Programs, Summary Presentation to Congress*, and reports of congressional hearings on aid.

88. G. Ranis and J. Nelson, *Measures to Ensure the Effective Use of Aid*, AID Discussion Paper No. 9, originally published in *Effective Aid*, ODI, 1966, p. 85.

In the same paper, it is explained that

In the long run, aid's 'influence potential' is much more important than its resource contribution. This is true for two reasons. Total aid from all sources has probably contributed roughly 20 per cent of total investment in the developing countries in the past few years. The use made of the remaining 80 per cent is clearly much more important in accelerating growth than is the use of aid alone. Furthermore, policies and procedures – import licensing arrangements, investment codes, marketing board pricing policies, power and transportation rate structures, tax provisions, to name only a few – affect economic development at least as powerfully as the presence or absence of adequate infrastructure or technical skills. Successful efforts to influence macro-economic and sectoral policies are likely to have a greater impact on growth than the added capital and skills financed by aid.[89]

The paper describes the development of 'techniques for using current aid negotiations to encourage specific self-help measures'. It distinguishes between 'the more general concept of influence' and 'the narrower concept of leverage'.

Leverage goes beyond influence and persuasion to condition aid, explicitly or implicitly, on specified host country action. Leverage may be positive or negative: aid may be withheld unless certain conditions are satisfied, or additional aid may be made available if the economic performance of the host country achieves specified standards. Positive leverage is sometimes called 'incentive programming'.

The paper further distinguishes between 'rewarding overall performance by generous aid allocations (thereby presumably encouraging continued good performance, and perhaps inducing other countries to improve their policies)', and 'using current aid negotiations to encourage specific

89. ibid., p. 91.

future self-help measures'. The 1961 Report of the President's Task Force on Foreign Assistance relied on the former, emphasizing the need to allocate aid between countries in such a way as to encourage 'good performance'. But since then the AID has increasingly turned its attention to the latter, partly no doubt because its own ability to determine the allocation of United States aid is small; at any rate the existing allocation is so clearly based on 'security' and political considerations that it is hardly such as to encourage 'good economic performance' as AID officials would probably define it.

Similar arguments on the need to 'match' higher levels of aid with 'better development policies' in Latin America and elsewhere have been advanced in AID Occasional Papers by Professor Hollis Chenery.[90] For instance he recommends that 'an effective system of aid administration' should concentrate on

(i) Relating the amount of total assistance to the size and effectiveness of the country's development programme in such a way as to induce maximum local efforts.

(ii) Supplying resources in the form best designed to support development priorities.

(iii) Using controls designed to enforce development priorities and efficient execution rather than to secure secondary benefits to the donor.[91]

Referring to 'slack economies with rising under-employment in Latin America', Chenery argues:

While no uniform relationship has been established between economic and political development, a strong case can be made

90. *Foreign Assistance and Economic Development* (with Alan Strout) and *Toward a More Effective Alliance for Progress*, published as AID Discussion Papers Nos. 7 and 13.

91. AID Discussion Paper No. 13, p. 32, published in March 1967, after Chenery had left the AID.

that democratic political development is much less likely to succeed without both rising income and a better distribution of its benefits among different groups in the population. If we take the more restricted objective of political stability rather than political and social development, there may be some counter-arguments against too rapid economic growth in primitive societies, but these hardly apply to the more sophisticated countries that comprise the bulk of Latin America.

He therefore argues that 'Development assistance should be systematically related to the effectiveness of local efforts (to achieve self-sustained growth).'[92]

The AID's major instrument for exercising 'leverage' is the system of conditional 'programme loans'.[93] Programme loans are tied to the purchase of goods in the United States and they may be tied to particular groups of commodities. They are not tied to specific uses in the country concerned; the counterpart funds generated from the sale of foreign exchange may be so tied but usually their use is more flexible than that of ordinary project loans. Countries receiving programme loans must however negotiate an agreement with the AID, which must be approved in

92. ibid., p. 29. Chenery left the AID in 1965 and also resigned, with its other members, from the Panel of Nine (see p. 25). He is critical of some current United States policies in Latin America. For example, on p. 32 of the above paper he says: 'Although attempts have been made in negotiating aid for Chile, Brazil, and Colombia to relate the amount of U.S. assistance to the country's performance, the principal criteria used have been measures of the country's success in overcoming short-run impediments to development, stabilization and reform. In order to achieve growth as well as stabilization, it is desirable to establish criteria for aid that are more specifically related to long-run development and which provide incentives to better economic performance.'

93. In Latin America the AID now makes programme loans to Brazil, Colombia and Chile. The idea of such programme loans was first developed not in the AID, but in the State Department proper.

Washington. The agreement, usually covering a period of one year, contains a number of general and some specific conditions on the economic and social policies to be adopted by the government receiving the loan. These conditions are embodied in a detailed and secret Loan Agreement between AID and the government concerned and also, in more general terms, in a Letter of Intent which in the case of a Latin-American country is formally addressed to the CIAP.[94] The loan is then disbursed in quarterly *tranches*, in theory according to whether the AID considers that the conditions have been satisfactorily observed. This method of providing finance has obvious advantages from the point of view of the government receiving it, since it can rapidly be disbursed and be used for the kind of imports for which external finance from official sources is not usually available. From the point of view of the AID, it provides considerable flexibility and disbursement can easily be delayed; whereas with project aid once a project has been agreed and started it is wasteful and difficult to stop it.[95] In countries where the AID does

94. See the next section of this chapter. CIAP takes no part in the negotiations. The Letters of Intent addressed to CIAP are not usually published but are somewhat less restricted and have on occasion been published (for example in the Gruening Report on Chile, cited chapter 1, note 13).

95. For a detailed discussion of programme loans see Andrzej Krassowski, *The Aid Relationship*, based on the American experience in Tunisia, ODI, 1968. See also Chenery, who says, for example: 'The matching principle has applications in aid administration in both project assistance and programme assistance. In the former, it is of less value because it simply requires a reallocation of existing government expenditures to supply the local share of a project's cost. While this indicates government support for that particular project, it is entirely compatible with inadequate total development efforts and falling rates of savings, as has been the case in several Latin American countries. When applied to a total programme of assistance, however,

not now make programme loans, the prospect of such loans, or of more project loans, can of course be held out as an inducement for the government to discuss its policies with the AID.

The possibility of such discussion is considerably increased by the existence in all Latin-American countries of permanent AID missions.[96] It is usually possible for the missions to establish a fairly continuous working relationship with the government of the country, involving discussion of general policies as well as of projects which the AID might finance, even when no programme loan is involved. The AID puts much faith in the idea of 'dialogue'. It claims, like the World Bank, that it is not a question of the AID 'imposing its ideas', but of 'finding the people with the right ideas' and, it is hoped, supporting them against internal opposition (thus presumably increasing their ability to impose their own and the AID's ideas). The AID also sometimes claims that the process of leverage does not imply increased intervention in the affairs of developing countries, but the mere fact of providing aid constitutes intervention since, unless strings are attached, it means supporting whatever the government in power wants to do.[97]

There are also some in the AID who attach more importance to regular discussion or negotiation with the

---

matching can be made much more effective. Programme assistance can be related to an overall development programme and made contingent on execution of policies designed to raise investment and to channel it into priority areas.' *Foreign Assistance and Economic Development*, AID Discussion Paper No. 7, p. 30.

96. These missions are sometimes very large: in Brazil the mission occupies about ten floors of an office block; the embassy is housed elsewhere.

97. See for example *Effective Aid*, ODI, 1966, Account of Proceedings, p. 34.

'right people' than to the programme loan system, involving as it does specific checking on policies and specific threats to cut aid. The AID is more flexible in negotiation than the World Bank or the IMF. On the whole, it is unwilling to make drastic breaks, to enforce exact observance of its conditions, to say 'take it or leave it'. It endeavours to maintain good relations with Latin-American governments and officials and it is more sensitive to political constraints. In practice, where programme loans have been agreed upon, it is rare for disbursement to be held up; the AID usually manages to agree that there were special circumstances which made it difficult for a particular condition to be observed. In any case programme loans usually cover so many different points that no one of them is likely to be important enough to affect disbursement on its own.

This flexibility might be expected to be an advantage, in the sense that it made AID's advice more acceptable to Latin Americans and AID officials more popular. But in fact the flexibility is to be accounted for not so much by the understanding and sympathy of AID officials as by the fact that the United States' reasons for supporting particular governments, whatever the AID may say or try to do, are more likely to be political than to have anything to do with whether or not their policies are conducive to development, or economic stability, or whatever other goals might have been set by the AID. The AID's ability to influence policies suffers from the fact that there is considerable confusion about what it is trying to achieve. From time to time it is expected to increase the provision of aid, or to threaten to cut it, for reasons unconnected with its views on the economic policies of the government concerned. The AID has little autonomy, and it must refer its decisions to Washington, where they may be overruled. It must argue its case for allocating particular amounts of aid to particular countries. Its programmes, designed to be embodied in programme loan agreements, are referred to Washington, where they are discussed and amended before they are finally approved as a basis for negotiation with the government concerned. In the case of Latin America, although not of other developing areas, the regional department of the AID in Washington is integrated into the regional department of the State Department proper; the AID local mission is officially under the authority of the United States ambassador.

It has been officially recognized, as a general precept, that the United States' foreign policy interests can be served through promoting development. But this does not mean that development considerations have priority in United States' decisions on aid and its allocation. The AID makes programme loans to three Latin-American countries: Brazil, Chile and Colombia. These countries do have rather sophisticated development programmes of which the AID is on the whole able to approve. Brazil is in some ways ideal from the AID's point of view, for it has a strong government with a strong stabilization policy, but there are also obvious political reasons for the United States to support the government which overthrew Goulart. Chile is more doubtful, for its programme has elements of which the I M F and the World Bank disapprove, so it is not clear how much the AID genuinely understands and approves and how much the United States has decided to support the Christian Democrats, come what may, as the only alternative to FRAP.[98] In Colombia similar doubts might occur: Colombia has a recent history of political disturbances as well as economic difficulties.

There are other sources of confusion. Some Latin

98. The Socialist–Communist coalition which nearly won the 1964 elections.

Americans say they 'always look for the trap' in AID offers of aid. The 'trap' can be that the United States wishes to supply some particular form of machinery for which it hopes to establish a market. More generally, some of the conditions attached to AID programme loans can be ambiguous; for example, the AID's particular enthusiasm for import liberalization programmes can be explained, as it usually is, in terms of the advantages for the country concerned; but it can also be explained, as many Latin Americans believe it should be, by the desire of the United States to promote its exports. More crudely, conditions are sometimes inserted in AID programmes which clearly have nothing to do with the promotion of the country's development and which involve the treatment of US private investors and concessions for US trading interests.[99] Put at their best, such efforts diminish the credibility of AID economists, and considerably reduce their effectiveness in negotiation.

Moreover, those 'development' policies which are supported by the AID must obviously conform with the United States' general political imperatives, and the definition of development varies. There was a time when the AID's involvement in general policies in Latin America was to some extent governed by the ideas of the Alliance for Progress, which were that if revolution was to be avoided, some reforms were essential. Among Alliance for Progress objectives there were many which were broadly social and of a distinctly 'progressive' nature, including targets for increasing taxation, presumably for developmental and social rather than anti-inflationary purposes, for land reform, education, housing and health. Most of these ideas have been dropped and only a few traces remain in the AID's current programmes. Among the conditions there is likely to

99. For a specific example see chapter 3, section on Peru, p. 146.

be something about education, and less frequently something about the distribution of income, even unemployment or land reform. In its project-lending the AID shows more concern with education and agriculture and with social objectives in general than the World Bank. As a whole, the idea of development promoted by the AID is still rather broader than that of the World Bank or the IMF.

Nevertheless, as the AID put it, the 'key' conditions in programme loans are now usually concerned with the exchange rate, the government's surplus on current account and with short-term financial and monetary policy in general. This has meant that in its more immediate and operational 'programme' concerns the AID has joined the other two agencies in their preoccupation with financial stability. Sometimes this takes the form of making AID lending conditional on agreement with the IMF. In some cases, especially where its mission has a strong group of economists, the AID makes it clear that some of the IMF's conditions are not important to it and there can be some difference in emphasis. For example, the AID may be more concerned than the IMF with an increase in government revenues. It is also true that the AID does not work as closely with the IMF as the World Bank does. But there is now a broad identity between the policies of the three institutions and a considerable degree of co-operation.

The adoption of this view of 'good performance' coincides with the disappearance of such official belief as there was in the possibility or desirability of United States-induced evolution and reform in Latin America. The United States government has actively encouraged and supported military dictatorships in Brazil and Argentina and its attitude towards the 'democracy in freedom' experiment in Chile has markedly changed. The obvious corollary of support for political stability and 'efficient' military governments is support for economic stabilization programmes. In the United States the change of attitude is sometimes explained by disillusion in the 'reformist' potentialities of Latin-American governments and in the possibility of rapid growth and stability. But there were always some obvious contradictions in Alliance for Progress objectives. The United States government expected Latin-American governments to reduce the privileges of some of their own nationals, for example through land reform and through a wider distribution of income. But it continued to exercise vigilant protection for the interests of United States private concerns, and thus in effect expected Latin-American governments to discriminate in favour of foreigners.[100]

100. See, for example, 'The Scandal of the Alliance for Progress', by a former State Department official, Simon G. Hanson, in *Life Magazine* of 13 January 1969; and see also 'The Alliance for Progress: the Sixth Year', by the same author, in *Inter-American Economic Affairs*, Vol. 22, No. 3, winter 1968. See especially pp. 13–16, on Brazil, in which Mr Hanson says for example: 'Mr Rusk said that "the substance of the Alliance for Progress has become the order of the day in Latin America". But if in this prime exhibit which would determine the success of the Alliance (i.e. Brazil), the elimination of democratic government, the reduction of the growth rate, the fatal crack-down on labor unions, the widening of the gap between the rich and the poor, the heavy decline in the standard of the mass of people, comprised the substance of the Alliance which emerged, then the original conception of the Alliance had been badly understood. And if in this prime exhibit, the pathetic surrender of decision-making authority to Washington and the cracking of the whip to force consent to objectives of direct investors whatever they might be and however inconsistent they might be with practice the continent over, constituted the substance of the Alliance, no Latin American country could possibly have known it at Punta del Este and still accepted participation in the Alliance' (p. 15); and: 'The decision-making power of Brazil had been wiped out to the

THE INTER-AMERICAN DEVELOPMENT BANK

The Inter-American Development Bank has so far resisted efforts to make it join the influencers of general policy. In the early days of the Alliance for Progress it was hoped that the IADB[101] would be an instrument for promoting Alliance for Progress aims. But it stuck to projects.

The IADB has had a somewhat different emphasis from the World Bank's in its project-lending. It has financed a number of projects in the economic infrastructure. But it has also financed projects in education and especially in housing, which has been a major field for IADB lending. It has been concerned with the problems of unemployment and '*marginalidad*' in expanding urban agglomerations. Whereas the few agricultural projects which the World Bank has financed have, with few exceptions, been irrigation projects or large commercial undertakings, the IADB has financed some more socially-orientated and sometimes fairly experimental projects in agriculture: for example, in Peru it is making unguaranteed loans in support of an attempt to revive the old communal forms of agriculture in the Inca uplands; in Chile it is lending for agrarian reform projects; in Colombia it is financing irrigation projects for *small*-holders. It is currently interested in promoting Latin-American integration and in financing regional projects. There are some who say that the IADB is taking excessive risks and that its loans will not be repaid.

---

great advantage particularly of foreign investors. The profit and loss statements, for instance, of such firms as Brazilian Light and Power Company, IT & T, American and Foreign Power Company, had become living monuments to the obedience which the Brazilians had consented to' (p. 14). See also chapter 4, note 30.

101. Or IDB or BID (Banco Interamericano de Desarrollo).

On the other hand, IADB, like the World Bank, insists on conditions designed to ensure the success of its projects. It is generally considered to be thorough in project preparation, nearly as insistent as the World Bank on feasibility studies, and it usually takes as long to negotiate conditions. It does work on a different principle. The World Bank does not sign the agreement for a loan until the project has been fully worked out and until it is satisfied that its conditions have been accepted; if it is not satisfied, the country may not get the loan. The IADB signs the agreement first and negotiates afterwards; the negotiations may be long and complicated, but the Bank has committed itself to make a loan in the end. It is possibly also true that the IADB, as a 'borrowers' organization',[102] is more flexible in negotiation than the World Bank, and that there is a somewhat greater sense of urgency and more sympathy for the need of Latin-American governments to show results.[103] But, as far as projects are concerned, the IADB has fully adopted the principle of negotiating on the use of its resources.

On general economic policies the IADB has been much more hesitant. At least until recently it has not attempted to make its lending conditional on judgements on governments' general policies, and it has not engaged in 'leverage' of the sort practised by the three main international agencies. It continued to lend in Brazil under Goulart; it continues to lend in Haiti, although not, of course, in Cuba. Efforts are fairly frequently made by the World Bank and by the United States to persuade it to put pressure on govern-

102. Voting-rights in the IADB are not weighted in proportion to the size of quotas (see *Annual Reports* of the IADB), and Latin Americans have a majority in voting.

103. Another reason for this flexibility is suggested by John White in an article, 'The Asian Development Bank: A Question of Style', *International Affairs*, Vol. 44, No. 4, October 1968.

ments. In a few cases recently it has shown signs of doing so: in Argentina a formal memorandum was presented to the Minister of Finance which had nothing to do with any IADB project and on another occasion, under pressure from the World Bank and the United States, the IADB agreed to 'suspend' its activities in Argentina, but without making recommendations. In Peru, in spite of such pressure, the Bank would do no more than talk informally to the financial authorities about the fiscal situation, and express concern whether enough revenue would be raised to cover the counterpart of IADB loans. In Paraguay the IADB has promoted the setting up of a development fund in the budget composed of taxes it had recommended, in the hope of ensuring that the counterpart funds for its loans would be available. In Costa Rica the IADB again joined the other international agencies in putting pressure on the government to apply an import surcharge under the provisions of the Central American Common Market. A more important move was the setting up of a consultative group for Ecuador; the IADB expressed its disapproval of recent Ecuadorean policies by refusing to call a meeting of the group; but it is a little doubtful about the effectiveness of a consultative group as a means of improving general policies (as opposed to project preparation and selection).

There are some in the IADB who would like to go further in this direction, including some who are fairly much in agreement with World Bank and IMF views on desirable policies in Latin America. Others would like to see CIAP taking over more of the role of vetting Latin-American policies, on the grounds that it would be better for this to be done by Latin Americans rather than by external agencies dependent on United States financial support and that, when the government concerned is represented in the discussions, there is a better chance that its political difficulties will be understood. The IADB already participates quite actively in CIAP reviews.

There are a number of reasons why the IADB has been reluctant to become involved in 'leverage'. Some of them are political; Bank officials with continuing political links in Latin America are sometimes hesitant about criticizing Latin-American governments. There are also doubts, as in the World Bank, about the effectiveness of loans being conditional on the adoption of policies unconnected with the projects financed by the IADB. There are feelings on the sovereignty of countries, and the right of governments to make their own decisions without external intervention. There are a number of people in the IADB who have doubts about the pretension of outsiders to know better; some, in particular, are highly critical of World Bank and IMF policies. Finally, it is sometimes maintained in the IADB, and in particular by its President Mr Felipe Herrera, that through its general policy pronouncements, its espousal of causes such as Latin-American integration, its research and studies, and its selection of sectors and projects for its loans, the IADB does in fact have an important influence on general policies in Latin America. But there is little sign in Latin America that the Bank's views on policies are taken into account or indeed noticed, except, of course, directly in connection with Bank projects.[104]

It seems clear that if the IADB does attempt to have a more direct influence on policies by basing its lending decisions on the adoption of particular policies, it will have to do so either by joining the ranks of the other international

104. For a very different view of the significance of the IADB, see John White, 'The Asian Development Bank: A Question of Style'; also his forthcoming ODI publication on regional development banks.

agencies, or, conceivably, through CIAP. It is unlikely that the IADB would be permitted to support policies which conflicted in any fundamental sense with those of the United States, or that it could do more in the way of defiance than refuse, as it now usually does, to support actively the policies of the United States and of the other international agencies.[105]

THE INTER-AMERICAN COMMITTEE FOR THE ALLIANCE FOR PROGRESS (CIAP)

The CIAP[106] exists, in spite of all that is said to the contrary, and is an interesting institution.

It was set up in 1963 as an organ of the IA–ECOSOC of the OAS,[107] after long discussion on whether it should have the power to *decide* on the allocation of aid under the Alliance for Progress, or merely to *advise* on its allocation. In the end the United States threatened not to participate if Latin Americans insisted on the CIAP 'deciding'. The CIAP's functions are therefore formally to study progress made in achieving Alliance for Progress objectives; to promote a greater multilateralization in the provision of aid; to make estimates of the financial resources needed and of their availability; to make reviews of Latin-American plans and make recommendations based on these reviews; to make proposals on the proportion of the necessary resources that should be provided from abroad. The CIAP now holds reviews, it is hoped annually, of each member country's performance, based on reports made by the

105. See also chapter 4, section on Alternative Policies in Aid.
106. The Spanish initials provide the usual abbreviation.
107. Inter-American Economic and Social Council of the Organisation of American States.

Secretariat.[108] These reviews are attended by representatives of CIAP and of the country concerned and, unofficially but regularly, by representatives of the World Bank, the IMF, the AID and the IADB. Also usually present are representatives of other international agencies, and occasionally some Europeans.

United States policy is said to be to try to strengthen the CIAP review process. The United States would like the CIAP to take a strong line on the economic policies of Latin-American countries; and it would like to involve Latin Americans in the process. Latin-American governments, although there is some rather resigned criticism of the fact that the CIAP has no power to affect the allocation of aid, nevertheless have taken the review process seriously, have submitted themselves to criticism, and have sent representatives of a high, usually ministerial, level. Reviews are seldom attended by representatives of Latin-American governments not directly concerned; but CIAP itself has strong Latin-American representation, and Dr Roberto Campos apparently attended a Chilean review at which interesting comparisons were made between Chilean and Brazilian policies. Those Latin Americans who are convinced that the tendency to base the provision of financial resources on 'performance criteria' is likely to grow sometimes express the hope that the CIAP will at least provide a more sympathetic hearing for their point of view. CIAP reports themselves are increasingly respected, although they are made, for the moment, with very small resources.

The idea of the CIAP Secretariat is that it should act as a kind of 'ombudsman' or mediator between Latin-American countries and the international agencies. In a sense, it is claimed, the fact that the CIAP is not a financial institution

108. CIAP reports are not published, but they are less restricted than IMF or World Bank reports.

is actually an advantage; it cannot be accused of using money as an instrument or of merely looking for bankable projects; it will be respected in so far as its judgements are serious and objective. The CIAP would like to be an agent transmitting pressures and preoccupations in each direction, explaining and trying to persuade. Usually it holds meetings before the review itself with the country concerned and with the international agencies.

An interesting feature of the CIAP is that it is critical both of Latin-American and of World Bank–IMF–AID policies. It must move cautiously in its criticisms.[109] But it would like, for instance, to 'educate' the IMF into a greater understanding of the non-financial aspects of development; to put the case for not reducing public expenditure; to put the problem of inflation in perspective; to demonstrate that 'sometimes orthodox remedies do not work'; to show that land reform in Peru is a 'pressing social problem' whereas in Argentina there is more of a need for economic efficiency; and perhaps especially to try to convince the financial community that everything is affected by the balance of payments and that the balance of payments itself is often affected by factors outside the control of Latin Americans.[110] The CIAP is attempting to develop a view of what 'good performance' means. Good

109. The attempt to incorporate the Panel of Nine into the CIAP was partly the result of the former's criticisms of United States policy.

110. See also, for example, an article by Walter J. Sedwitz, Executive Secretary of CIAP, in the *Journal of Commerce*, April 1968, in which he says: 'Can the United States continue to tell Latin America that it must become more competitive, that it must lower its trade barriers, and that it must allow freer play to market forces, if these principles are not practiced at home? Is it possible for this country to expect the Latin American nations to launch massive new efforts at export promotion, if the chances are that as soon as these efforts show promise of success, entry into the US market may be closed?'

performance in relation to what? Is the Brazilian performance 'good'? There was much understanding and sympathy for the alternative policies tried in Chile. There is also questioning of the tendency to evaluate performance in measurable results: growth of output, public savings, price stability, and so on. It might, it is felt, be more important that a country was making a big effort to organize itself or to transform its institutions, or even that it was conducting a social revolution. Are Guatemala and Nicaragua, with high rates of growth, price stability, no structural change and social tensions of an extreme variety, performing well? The World Bank and the IMF think they are. The CIAP questions.

Whether CIAP questioning is likely to have any effect is another matter. The CIAP feels that its influence on countries, if it has the weight of the financial institutions behind it, can be considerable. It feels also that the IMF and the World Bank 'cannot withstand criticism indefinitely'. But the CIAP's criticism may be no more effective than anybody else's; the World Bank and the IMF do not, for the moment, take it very seriously. The weight of the CIAP, so long as it is given no power over the allocation of resources, is little more than moral.

Chapter 3

APPLICATION

THIS chapter will try to give some idea of how the organizations described above work in practice, by describing some of the things which were happening early in 1967 in the four countries I went to: Colombia, Chile, Brazil and Peru.

Total accuracy is impossible. The negotiations of the World Bank, the IMF and the AID are conducted in great secrecy. Some of the things I was told were flatly contradictory. But I was told enough, by people involved in both sides of negotiations and also by outsiders, to have some idea of what was happening.

COLOMBIA

At the end of 1966 Colombia had a crisis with the international agencies. On 29 November President Lleras appeared on television to announce that he was not going to devalue the peso because foreigners told him to, that he was breaking off negotiations with the IMF, and that he was imposing drastic controls. These included stopping dealings in foreign exchange for two days, after which all dealings would be subject to central bank control, putting commercial payments at the bottom of the list of priorities, and returning to a tight system of import controls.

Colombia has had a long and on the whole close relationship with the World Bank, except for a period under the populist government of Rojas Pinilla, from 1956–8, when the Bank stopped making commitments to lend. The first Bank mission was to Colombia, in 1948, under Lauchlin

Currie.[1] The report made a general economic appraisal; for the first time in Colombia it discussed national income, the balance of payments and such concepts; and it recommended the construction of a railway and roads. The Bank has been a big lender in Colombia, mainly for railways, roads and electric power, and the country has been the third biggest recipient of its loans in Latin America, after Mexico and just after Brazil. In 1965 one of the first four of the Bank's consultative groups was set up in Colombia. The World Bank remains there the acknowledged 'chairman' of the international agencies. The Americans became interested in the country at the time when the *violencia* appeared likely to cause major disruption and perhaps revolution, and subsequently when, mainly because of falling coffee prices, Colombia had increasing difficulties with its balance of payments. The AID has been making programme loans since 1963. Colombia has also been using IMF facilities for some years. The involvement of the international agencies was thus substantial, and by the mid-sixties considerable amounts of aid were being received. In August 1966, under Colombia's system of four-year alternation between the Liberal Party and the Conservative Party, the Liberals came into power under President Lleras Restrepo. President Lleras, an economist with liberal inclinations, had a strong commitment to reforms; but, as usual, he faced powerful conservative opposition.

Under the previous government, in November 1965, Colombia, at that time in considerable economic difficulties,

1. Who now lives in Colombia and subsequently became critical of the policies of the international agencies. See Lauchlin Currie, *Accelerating Development, the Necessity and the Means*, McGraw-Hill, 1966. The 1948 World Bank mission's report was published under the title *The Basis of a Development Program for Colombia*, International Bank for Reconstruction and Development, Washington, 1950.

had made a stand-by agreement for $36·5 million over one year with the IMF. The international agencies had said they would suspend their aid until the situation was improved. Finally, a new Finance Minister was appointed, the peso was devalued in September, and in November the government agreed with the IMF on a series of measures which were supposed to be conducive to a more favourable investment climate and, while not 'de-emphasizing' long-term development objectives, to reduce the likelihood of recurrent financial crises. These measures included commitments to embark on a major policy of import liberalization and to rely more exclusively on changes in the exchange rate, by shifting imports from one exchange category to another in order to regulate the level of imports; to achieve current budget surpluses of specified amounts by increasing revenues and cutting current expenditures; to limit borrowing from the Central Bank to specified amounts, and within these ceilings to restrict the availability of credit for coffee production; and to relate wage and salary increases to productivity increases. In addition the IMF, apparently not confident of the efficacy of these measures, demanded that Colombia accept balance of payments targets over the year: if Colombia failed to meet these targets, even if it had observed the IMF's conditions, then the IMF reserved the right to withdraw or not to renew its stand-by.

By the autumn of 1966 it was becoming clear that Colombia was going to fail the balance of payments test. It seems that the other conditions of the agreement were more or less fully carried out. There are one or two claims to the contrary; but the most authoritative version is that Colombia fulfilled all the IMF's conditions on limitations in the money supply, government expenditure cuts and revenue increases, coffee policy, import liberalization, and devaluation of the exchange rate on some categories of goods. The government also went further in import liberalization than was stipulated in the agreement; Lleras himself made some sharp moves towards liberalization immediately after he came to power. But this was a subject for congratulation rather than for blame from the IMF and the AID, who at any rate could not be expected to object to any measures of import liberalization and who agreed with the Colombian government's view that imports should be very largely liberalized so as to discover what their true level was likely to be. Imports certainly were at a high level, unnervingly so, it seemed, in the autumn of 1966; but it subsequently became clear that their level was not above the level projected at the time of the 1965 agreement.

The main trouble was that Colombia's receipts from coffee were less than expected; both the prices and the volume of Colombia's exports fell, the latter partly because of cuts in Colombia's quota, partly because of lack of demand for the high-quality mild coffee produced by Colombia. The estimates of the 1966 'shortfall' vary from Colombian estimates of $70 million and an AID estimate of $60 million to much lower IMF estimates.[2] Other subsidiary explanations are produced: for instance, that Colombia was unable to use AID funds and other tied foreign exchange once it had liberalized its import system. But, as was stated in an AID apologia for the policies of the international agencies, the fall in coffee receipts 'would be enough to explain anything'.

Whatever the cause, by the autumn of 1966, the balance of payments situation was disturbing. IMF and World Bank missions went to Colombia. These, together with members of the AID permanent mission, met at the US embassy and decided that devaluation was necessary. The

2. Colombia finally got $18·9 million from the IMF in compensatory finance (see below).

IMF representative went to the Colombian government
and said that the IMF would not renew its stand-by unless
Colombia devalued, apparently also making plain by what
amount this should be. The New York commercial banks
stopped lending. At this time Colombia was also negotiating for a new programme loan from the United
States; according to one AID version, the United States
had already made plain in August that it was not prepared
to provide 'advance commodity financing', but only to
commit itself to reimburse Colombia, up to a certain
amount, after proof had been given of commodities imported from the United States; this would have meant that
immediate funds would not have been available whether or
not agreement with the IMF had been reached. Whatever
the truth of this,[3] negotiations for any kind of programme
loan were broken off after Lleras's television announcement, on 29 November, of his refusal to devalue at the
behest of the IMF. The World Bank, since this is not its
policy, did not stop disbursements on its project loans; but
the question of calling a meeting of the consultative group
was postponed. Colombia did not devalue, and in his
television broadcast Lleras announced the reversal of the
import liberalization policy.

There are conflicting explanations as to why all this
happened. The first question is on whose initiative the IMF
representative was acting. There are some, in the AID
especially, who profess to believe that the IMF pushed for
devaluation on its own initiative and was responsible for the
break by being excessively rigid in negotiation; the AID, it
is said, would have been more flexible. According to one
AID version, neither they nor the World Bank foresaw the
crisis; they believed that the IMF would be understanding
about the reasons for Colombia's failure of the balance of

3. See below.

payments test, and the AID had reserved the right to dissociate itself from the IMF if it called for devaluation; thus after Lleras's television appearance they had had to make the decision not to do so in a hurry. There were also some doubts expressed in the AID about the wisdom of the policy of devaluation. There were many in Colombia who believed that there was some possibility that the AID or the World Bank might in fact dissociate itself from the IMF and continue to discuss future lending policies or the calling of the consultative group, whether or not Colombia reached agreement with the IMF. And there was near-universal criticism of the manner in which the IMF made its decisions known to the Colombian government and its failure to take account of national susceptibilities. On the other hand, it was said by others in the AID that the United States was always fully behind the IMF and that at worst the negotiations were clumsily conducted. One IMF version of the story was that the United States embassy took the initiative, inviting the IMF and World Bank missions to the embassy and saying it was time to be tough on the Colombian government. According to this story, the IMF representative merely acted as spokesman (or scapegoat), following instructions from the United States embassy and Washington. The World Bank, however, in spite of the views current in Colombia, was fully behind devaluation and also probably felt more strongly than the IMF that pressure should be put on the Colombian government. It was the World Bank which 'told' the New York banks to stop lending in Colombia.

The next question is why the international agencies decided devaluation was necessary. Many Colombians, officially and unofficially, maintained that it was not necessary, and that Colombia could have survived the balance of payments crisis without devaluing if the IMF had been prepared to renew its stand-by, if the AID had agreed to make disbursements immediately on another programme loan, if the New York banks had not stopped lending, if the IMF had immediately provided compensatory finance for the shortfall in coffee earnings, or if only some of these things had happened. Some people in the AID definitely supported this view. From the political point of view, had this been possible the advantages for Lleras would have been considerable. Devaluation in Colombia is extremely unpopular and has in the past given rise to general strikes. Lleras, in his first public appearance as President, had given a pledge that he would not employ this measure. The economic arguments against devaluation were more controversial. First: unless a government is politically strong, no economic policy is likely to be successful; decisions about devaluation can seldom be purely 'technical'. Second: there were doubts about the wisdom of Colombia's continual devaluations; in the past they had tended to set off rounds of price increases and wage demands,[4] while doing little to help exports, since the price of coffee is fixed outside Colombia and the possibility of immediate expansion in other exports is small. It was also argued that since Colombia had had controls, especially on the import of luxury goods, more or less continuously since the war, devaluation on its own was almost certain to be inadequate as a means of reducing

4. For example, in December 1962 the peso was devalued by 34 per cent. The following year the rate of inflation was 45 per cent, whereas in the previous five years it had averaged 6 per cent. This was 'essentially as a response to the devaluation. The fiscal situation, for example, was considerably better in 1963 than it had been during the preceding year.' See United Nations Economic Commission for Latin America, *Economic Survey of Latin America 1964*, New York, 1966, p. 55. See also Eduardo Wiesner Durán, 'Las Modificaciones del Tipo de Cambio y los Niveles Domésticos de Precios', in *La Nueva Economía*, Bogotá, May 1966.

imports; Colombians would be willing to pay very high prices for imported goods once direct controls were removed. Devaluation was also opposed by some of those who believed in the policy of import liberalization, as the Lleras government clearly did. These people hoped to discover what the 'normal' level of imports would be after the immediate rush for imports caused by the measures of liberalization. There were signs that imports were levelling off; it also seemed that importers who were stockpiling luxury goods in the expectation of devaluation or controls had nearly reached their limit, and it had been hoped that they could be discouraged from future speculation by a refusal of the government to succumb to pressures to change its policies. Moreover the level of prices in terms of dollars in Colombia is quite low, considerably lower than in some other Latin-American countries.

Why then did the international agencies want to force Colombia into devaluation? The agencies may have been right in arguing that devaluation was necessary simply in order to keep up with the price increases over the year; they may even have been right in believing that the balance of payments crisis was bound to force Colombia into devaluation or reversal of its policies; certainly their actions made Colombia's position untenable, since it possessed no reserves. In the World Bank it was said, rightly or wrongly, that at the time of the 1965 stand-by it had not been possible to persuade the government to devalue as far as the international agencies had thought desirable; this was why they insisted on the balance of payments guarantee. In any case, the agencies, with or without thorough consideration of the political and economic implications, proceeded to decide that devaluation was necessary, and by how much, and to attempt to impose their decision on Colombia.

Finally, there is the question why Lleras took such dramatic action on 29 November. The cabinet met all night before the decision was taken to defy the international agencies and to impose controls. The explanations given by Colombians and in the international agencies were mainly political and personal. There were not many who claimed that Lleras himself was, for economic reasons, against devaluation, and in favour of controls. He would no doubt have liked, from every point of view, to carry through the policy of liberalization. He may have thought devaluation necessary; what is certain is that he would in any case have preferred to devalue in his own way and at his own time. Possibly he would have devalued in a gradual and fairly concealed way – as, in fact, was already happening with categories of imports being moved from one exchange rate to another – rather than the across-the-board devaluation on which the IMF insisted. Certainly he would have tried to choose the moment for devaluation, if he devalued at all, so that the political and economic repercussions were minimized.[5]

The political explanations given by the international agencies tended to be cruder. They professed disappointment in Lleras's toughness and dedication to economic principles, which they had believed, they said, to be greater. Personal explanations, of a more or less petty kind, were also advanced. It was for instance claimed that Lleras deliberately pretended not to know that the AID and the World Bank had always been behind the IMF. On 25

5. See also C. P. Kindleberger, 'Liberal policies versus controls in the foreign trade policies of developing countries', AID Discussion Paper No. 14, Washington, 1967, on devaluation in India, in which the author makes clear the importance of the circumstances surrounding devaluation, including commitment by the government concerned, and argues that these were unfavourable in India.

November, at a time when his relations with the IMF were already deteriorating, Lleras spoke confidently on television of the support his policies were receiving from the World Bank and the AID. It was suggested that his advisers knew that their support was dependent on his agreeing with the IMF. On 29 November he said that one of the reasons for his actions was that he had just discovered that the AID was not, after all, prepared to provide advance commodity financing. It was said that he had always known this; any other belief was 'wishful thinking', at best. Others in the AID felt that Lleras could not have known the AID's position, expressed regrets that the AID should have 'sprung it on him', and suggested that Lleras acted out of pique when he discovered that the international agencies were solidly together. Others blamed the IMF for undiplomatic presentation of its demands. In the World Bank, it was said that Lleras disliked discovering that he was bound by an international agreement made by his predecessor.

Dislike of the deviousness of the international agencies' behaviour may conceivably have played some part in Lleras's decision to break off negotiations. Possibly also Lleras wanted to demonstrate to the international agencies that he was not prepared to have his policies dictated to him, and to ensure that in future he was treated with more respect. But it is doubtful how significant these personal explanations were. Of far greater importance were internal political considerations of a rather different sort from those suggested by the international agencies. Lleras gained considerable popularity from his defiance of the international agencies and his announcement that Colombia would go it alone. It was suggested by a Colombian official that Lleras lacked mystique, and that this demonstration of independence and toughness was very good for him. As in other places and times, the international agencies had served a useful purpose, from the point of view of the government, not at all by pushing towards 'sensible' policies, but by providing something to fight against, a means of gaining relatively easy popularity.

After this crisis, fence-mending operations began. The AID and the World Bank, whose part in the IMF's decisions was still not fully realized by the Colombians, acted as 'mediators'. There were still doubts whether the Bank would 'dissociate' itself from the IMF. In December the World Bank gave a press conference in which it praised Lleras. In January 1967 a World Bank mission came to Colombia to discuss the possibility of re-opening negotiations with the IMF, ostensibly to bring the two sides together. After this, the Colombian government agreed to talk to the IMF. Another IMF mission, with a different head, came in February. This time the Americans put pressure on the IMF *not* to be tough. In April an agreement was announced.

Lleras claimed that, with the help of the good offices of the World Bank, he had persuaded the IMF to accept a Colombian programme. The agreement in fact was a compromise between the Colombian government and the international agencies. Lleras, in a way, did quite well. He got a stand-by from the IMF and a programme loan from the AID, with five months' delay, but with his popularity in Colombia much increased. The agreement with the IMF allowed him to keep the import controls; he made no specific commitment on liberalization; although he agreed to a floating exchange rate, whether the rate floated downwards would depend on how much he decided to relax the controls. The IMF got the (theoretically) floating exchange rate; it also got a commitment to a very tight credit policy; but it had no means of ensuring that money supply, however limited, was not ahead of growth, since this would depend on how many imports the Colombian government allowed. The stand-by has been variously described as 'botched' and 'fuzzy'. It is, to say the least, doubtful whether this sort of swapping of 'concessions' is the best way to determine a country's economic policy.

It may be that the Colombian case is an unfortunate exception, a question of bad negotiation and clash of personalities which happened to become fairly public, and therefore was made more acute, as a result of particular political circumstances. The possibility of this sort of confusion is not the most important reason for having doubts about the international agencies' desire to influence general policies. It nevertheless illustrates what can happen when there is a government whose economic policies are not completely clear, but which is not willing to have policies dictated to it, and in any case has political difficulties with which probably it alone is competent to deal.

There is also, of course, another and wider aspect of this débâcle. This is the question whether, from the point of view of long-term economic development, the international agencies were right in what they were trying to achieve. This will be discussed in chapter 4. But Colombia provides an illustration of almost exclusive concentration on the exchange rate, very little regard for long-term or supply problems, and rather indiscriminate pressing of some policies which were likely to have an adverse effect in the long term.[6] Even as far as short-term policies were concerned, there are some signs that decisions which were

6. For instance, there was apparently no attempt to ensure that Colombia's tight credit policies did not excessively damage agricultural prospects; since credit for imports is the easiest and most popular form of credit, global credit restrictions have to be very tight indeed before imports are affected.

important from Colombia's point of view were made with rather inadequate care and thought.[7]

CHILE

Structuralist ideas on economics[8] as usually propounded purport to provide an alternative to orthodox or monetarist ideas without drastically changing the constitutional framework. They offer proposals for a programme of expansion and redistribution of income, involving gradual changes in the structure of the economy, to provide the possibility of durable and stable growth. They oppose deflationary policies of the IMF variety on the grounds that they hurt the poorer sections of the population and that they inhibit growth and the restructuring of the economy. It is arguable that the Frei government was trying to apply these ideas in its first two or three years in office (1964–7). It appeared that it might have found a middle way in economics, as in politics, between stagnation and revolution. Its economic policies had some unorthodox features which at first seemed to be rather successful. The fact that their success was short-lived may possibly prove that the international agencies are, in one sense, right; there is no painless way of solving Chile's economic problems, without somebody's interests being hurt. The question, of course, is *whose* interests are hurt.

Inflation in Chile had been more or less continuous since the end of the nineteenth century. After the Second World

7. See also Richard L. Maullin, 'The Colombia–IMF disagreement of November–December 1966: an interpretation of its place in Colombian politics', Memorandum RM–5314–RC, Rand Corporation, 1967.

8. See chapter 2, note 24, and chapter 4, pp. 163–4.

War, stabilization programmes of the orthodox variety were tried on several occasions, with impermanent effects.[9] In 1963 and 1964 the Alessandri government was attempting to control inflation with the help of stand-by agreements with the IMF and programme loans from the AID, which on this occasion provided the main pressure for stabilization. Chile ran big balance of payments deficits and its foreign debt rose rapidly.[10] Alessandri's strategy was to borrow from abroad and pay for this out of the growth it was hoped to generate. Apart from this, efforts were concentrated on keeping wage and salary increases below the rise in the cost of living and on limiting government expenditure; admittedly they were not very successful efforts. At any rate, in 1963 and 1964 growth was barely equal to the population increase; the rate of inflation in 1964 was 38 per cent.

The Frei government came into office in September 1964. The economic authorities, and especially the Finance Minister Molina, had clear views on policy. Their control and knowledge of the economy was more effective and sophisticated than under the previous government. Their economic programme had several structuralist features.[11]

9. See for example David Felix, 'Structural Imbalances, Social Conflict and Inflation: an appraisal of Chile's recent anti-inflationary effort', *Economic Development and Cultural Change*, January 1960; A. O. Hirschman, *Journeys towards Progress*, Anchor Books, Doubleday & Co., Inc., New York, 1965, pp. 215–98.

10. From 1960 to 1964 the Chilean balance of payments deficits amounted to $520 million, and the foreign currency debt rose from $800 million to $1,800 million. See ECLA Report on Latin America for 1966, E/CN.12/767/Add.1.

11. This has been disputed. For example it was claimed by the AID (see below) that the programme merely reinforced the classic anti-inflationary policies pursued under the Alessandri government. On the other hand it has also been claimed that the programme followed closely the ideas set out in Osvaldo Sunkel's article, 'Inflation in Chile:

The most important general principle of the programme was the intention *simultaneously* to achieve three objectives: to slow down inflation, to increase the rate of growth and to redistribute income in a progressive direction. The government's emphasis on agrarian reform reflected these objectives. They were considered not to be alternatives, as monetarists might argue, but conditions of one another, both for political and for economic reasons.

The government was concerned as a major objective with the elimination of inflation. It was not prepared to try to achieve stabilization in the short run. The authorities conceded that it would be technically possible to achieve stabilization without growth, but from the political point of view it was considered impossible. And from the economic point of view, it was felt that the results were unlikely to be maintained: as soon as growth began again, all the old problems would recur, basically because nothing had been done to ensure that supply would be any more likely to keep up with demand than it had in the past. The Government claimed that it was attacking not merely the symptoms but also the 'fundamental causes of inflation'.[12] In other words it was tackling the failure of the economy to grow, and in particular the stagnation of agriculture and the difficulty in expanding Chile's exports.

The authorities also agreed with the monetarist point of view to the extent of believing that stabilization programmes in the past had failed partly because governments had been politically unable to carry them through. Thus part of the sophistication of their policy was that they calculated rather carefully where the burden of readjustment was to fall. This

---

an Unorthodox Approach', *International Economic Papers*, No. 10 (also in *El Trimestre Económico*, octubre–diciembre 1958).

12. See Christian Democrat Manifesto, 1966.

was done by compensating workers for rises in agricultural prices by a fairly liberal wages policy,[13] and devaluing the escudo by monthly adjustments, slowly at first, thus to some extent avoiding the all-round price increases which had usually followed devaluation in the past.

As far as growth was concerned, the government decided to concentrate as an immediate objective on an expansion in copper production and exports. Successive Chilean governments had tried, through incentives such as tax reductions and devaluation, to get the US copper companies to produce and export more. The Frei government made an agreement with the copper companies under which they were to double production by 1970; it undertook to provide most of the capital, and obtained a loan for this purpose from the US Export-Import Bank. Other industrial projects were supported through the State-owned CORFO[14]: petro-chemicals, paper, a sugar refinery, cellulose. In addition government expenditure, both current and investment, expanded considerably, particularly in education; although there were also big tax increases, the budgetary deficit at first increased. The industrial sector, which had much unutilized capacity, apparently was able to expand production to meet the increase in demand and the shift in its pattern; some producers of mass-consumption goods in particular increased their overall profits, in spite of bigger wage and tax bills and reasonably effective price controls, as a result of a bigger volume of sales.

A major policy of the Frei government was land reform. Like other policies in the government's programme, it was

13. The principle was adopted that wages should rise at the same rate as the rise in the cost of living; in addition, preferential increases above this rate were granted to the lowest-paid workers, particularly in agriculture.

14. Corporación de Fomento de la Producción.

supposed to serve several purposes – anti-inflationary, productive, redistributive and social. According to structuralist theories one of the main causes of inflation is the slow growth of food supplies. Chilean agriculture is inefficient, and a number of large farms are under-utilized. It was considered that changes in the system of land tenure would not only improve material and social conditions for the rural poor but also increase production, in many cases immediately. It seems that production on the land expropriated in the first years of the Frei government did in fact increase, although the government was not particularly successful in expanding the general level of agricultural production. On farms which were not expropriated, output also sometimes rose, since their owners hoped to escape expropriation in this way, although there appears also to have been some precautionary disinvestment. The government's land-reform law, which was held up in Congress for over two years, made expropriation somewhat easier and the terms for landlords somewhat less favourable.

In addition, the government had a number of other policies of a social and redistributory nature. As has been said, the government's expenditure, current as well as investment, increased considerably. The land-reform law allowed peasants to organize themselves in trade unions, which had previously been banned. The minimum wage in rural areas was raised. Educational programmes were expanded and reformed. It was claimed that, with its programme of '*promoción popular*', the government was laying the foundation for a 'communitarian' form of society. Unemployment was reduced. In general, the government's fiscal policies, its policies on wages and prices, and its success in reducing unemployment, constituted what the I M F described as 'a sharp redistribution of income'; and the redistribution in fact went further than had been planned.

All this did amount to considerable innovation along what might be described as structuralist lines. In the first two years it also seemed a rather triumphant vindication of structuralist arguments on growth and inflation. Chile achieved the hat-trick: more growth, less inflation, and some progressive redistribution of income. In 1965 the rate of growth was 5 per cent and the rate of inflation was down to 26 per cent. In 1966, growth was 7 per cent, inflation 17 per cent.[15] In 1967, inflation was planned to be 10 per cent.[16] Chile also greatly improved its balance of payments position; in 1966 it had a record balance of payments surplus of $100 million. Commercial arrears were paid off; the proportion of short-term high interest debt in Chile's total foreign debt declined considerably. For 1967 the government was able to decide to do without the AID programme loan[17] and the IMF stand-by.

But much of this success was made possible by high copper prices. In 1965, copper prices increased by 11 per cent, which accounted for most of the export increase of 15 per cent; in 1966 copper prices increased by 25 per cent, total exports by a third. The share of copper in Chile's total exports increased from 60 per cent in 1964 to nearly 70 per cent in 1966. Increases in copper prices are said to have accounted for half the increase in tax receipts. The government maintained that it could have adjusted its programme to a lower level of copper prices without distorting it, and that it would, in any case, have been possible to obtain aid in comparable amounts if copper prices had

15. These are official government figures; their accuracy is frequently questioned; in particular the figures given for 'rate of inflation' are based on a retail price index composed, in principle, of mass-consumption goods.

16. But see below.

17. But in October the government accepted a programme loan of $15 million, to be disbursed during the last quarter of 1967.

not risen. But the fact that copper prices fell in 1967, although they were still high, must be at least partly responsible for the government's failure to continue the slowing down of inflation in 1967 and 1968.[18] It also of course contributes to the force of one of the structuralists' main arguments: that the difficulties of developing countries are to a considerable extent caused by fluctuations in their export prices and deterioration, especially during the 1950s, in their terms of trade.

More serious perhaps from a theoretical point of view is that the Chilean government, like other governments trying to achieve stabilization, quite rapidly found itself faced with the difficulty of increasing investment. By 1967, existing capacity in the private sector was being fully used and new investment was needed for expansion. The limits in taxation had, in the government's view, been reached or possibly exceeded. There were some who felt that taxation must be reduced in order to allow the private sector to invest. The government resorted to a highly controversial alternative: wage-earners, instead of receiving their full wage adjustment in cash in proportion to the rise in the cost of living, were to receive part of it in the form of bonds conferring ownership in new industries to be set up by the government. The government claimed that, faced with the alternatives of a reduction in the level of investment or a reduction in the level of taxation of the private sector, it had adopted a solution that would reduce the concentration of industrial power; the proposal could in fact be interpreted as quite radical, leading to workers' ownership of state industries. But it was strongly attacked by the left, who saw

18. In 1967 the rate of inflation was 21·9 per cent and in 1968 it was back to 27·9 per cent, in spite of some efforts, especially towards the end of the year, to tighten up price controls on items which weighed heavily in the index, and some holding over of price increases into 1969.

it as undermining the standards of living of the workers and felt that the bonds were likely to become worthless. The policy had to be abandoned amid political crisis, rather like IMF policies before it. Since, in an effort to prevent the increase in the rate of inflation, the government also decided on restrictions in government expenditure and in the expansion of credit in 1968, many of the expansionist aspects of the government's economic policies were abandoned.

In general, it could be argued that the government's policies were too cautious, and they were quite unrevolutionary. This is particularly apparent in the case of the two major planks of the government's political programme: 'Chileanization' of the copper companies, and land reform. As far as the copper companies were concerned, the government, like other governments before it, made big concessions to the copper companies in order to get them to agree to expand their production. The companies got a large reduction in their rate of taxation. 'Chileanization' meant basically that the Chilean government put up most of the capital for expansion. In one case it bought a majority share in a company's capital, but acquired comparatively little management control. The copper companies were delighted with the arrangement. From an economic point of view Chile would almost certainly have gained if the companies had simply been nationalized.[19] After their long and fruitful exploitation of Chile's mineral resources, and with Chile's almost total dependence on their activities, the copper companies no doubt know that they will, one day, be nationalized. As an interim arrangement, the Frei government's 'Chileanization' is a great boon.

The land-reform programme originally aimed at the

19. See for example Keith Griffin, *Under-development in Spanish America*, Allen and Unwin, 1969.

settling of 100,000 families on expropriated land by 1970. This would have been about 40 per cent of the existing landless population. Partly because it was over two years before the government's new law was passed by Congress, the programme was slow in starting. By 1967, about 5,000 families had been settled. It became clear that the target would be reduced. The main justification used for reducing it was that the programme would be too expensive. About a third of the cost was for compensation of land-owners; although much of this was in fixed-term bonds, and therefore involved an element of expropriation, it could be argued that it was further compressible. The rest was for new housing and roads, machinery, working capital, education and research. The government was determined that the programme should be thorough and that great efforts should be made to avoid a drop in production. But it is possible that part of its determination arose from the fact that it underestimated the capabilities of Chilean peasants, and that it failed to distinguish between what was essential and what, like government housing, was not. Possibly the government's determination also arose from the fact that the Cabinet, most of whom were land-owners, had their own reasons for time-consuming thoroughness. Moreover, when land is transferred there is likely to be some fall in production on some farms, and certainly some increase in local consumption, however cautious the programme, before the undeniable and undenied long-term benefits of land reform are translated into higher marketed production. Other things being equal, therefore, the sooner the land is transferred, the sooner these benefits are likely to materialize. Also, if the period of transfer is short, one of the arguments advanced by the critics of land reform, that uncertainty about ownership causes land-owners not to invest, disappears.

127

What of the attitude of the international agencies? First it should be said that it is clear that one of the reasons why the copper companies, at least, were not nationalized, and why the Christian Democrats were elected rather than the FRAP, the Communist-Socialist coalition committed to nationalization, was fear of the United States. Before the 1964 election, the Christian Democrats had come to an understanding with the United States government on various issues, including treatment of the copper companies. This was one reason why the United States decided to back them. In the absence of such an agreement, or had the Christian Democrats been defeated by the FRAP, the United States would have had various means of retaliation at its disposal. The economic ones might not have been decisive. Forgoing aid and foreign private investment, nationalizing United States assets, and defaulting on debts could have had major economic advantages for Chile, and would presumably not have led to the loss of the 85 per cent of Chile's markets for copper which are in Europe. But it was clear that the United States would have gone, and still would go, to considerable lengths, including possibly military intervention, perhaps through the intermediary of the Chilean army or of other Latin-American governments, to prevent a party or coalition committed to nationalization and radical social changes from winning the elections, or, if it did, from taking office, or at least from putting its policies into effect.

Once the Christian Democrats were elected, with their commitment to 'revolution in liberty', the IMF and the AID were again involved.[20] A Chilean mission went to Washington to negotiate a new stand-by with the IMF. A programme loan was negotiated with the AID. A re-

20. On the relationship between the AID and the Chilean authorities, see a forthcoming ODI study by Philip O'Brien.

scheduling of Chile's debts was arranged, mainly on the insistence of the United States government. The World Bank was not directly involved in negotiations on Chile's general economic policies during this period, although it made a large loan for electric power in 1966; but it too expressed its views on Chilean policies and its mission in Chile in 1966 wrote a general report.

The attitude of the international agencies to the Frei government's economic programme was interesting. It consisted mainly in trying to ensure that Chilean policies were 'consistent' with one another. A US State Department view was that the Chileans had a confused set of policies which were not internally consistent, and that programme loan negotiations in the first year had forced Chile to reconcile the conflicting objectives of simultaneous income redistribution and reduction in inflation. There appeared to be very little recognition of, or willingness to discuss, the theories behind Chilean policies, particularly the theory that the government's objectives, far from being 'inconsistent', were in fact conditional on one another. A notable exception to this failure of understanding was in the AID mission in Chile, where, at least in one case, there was considerable sympathy with and understanding for Chilean economic and social objectives. Elsewhere officials were prepared to admit, at most, that the Chilean authorities, with strong left-wing opposition, were justified in their concern with political support. There was also some recognition of practical successes. The IMF's 1967 *Annual Report*, for instance, began with a laudatory paragraph on Chile's achievement of faster growth, slower inflation, improvement in the balance of payments and sharp redistribution of income. The AID was of course prepared to admire some of the government's social policies *per se*. The World Bank's report was more negative.

At any rate, the IMF and the AID decided, with reservations, to give full financial backing to the government's programme. The United States had essential political reasons for supporting the Christian Democrats, whatever their policies. In so far as the IMF and some US officials praised the government's initial economic successes, they tended[21] to ascribe these to what was felt to be a more vigorous application of the kinds of anti-inflationary policies which the two agencies had rather unsuccessfully been trying to persuade the Alessandri government to adopt. The AID was particularly pleased by, and apparently felt with very dubious justification responsible for, the government's achievement in increasing tax revenues and reforming the budget. The IMF was encouraged by some relaxation and simplification of import and exchange controls, and by the 'considerable reduction in the rate of overall credit expansion'. Both in the IMF and in the AID there was praise for improvement in the techniques of monetary control. But there is little doubt that they also accepted aspects of the programme of which they disapproved, or at any rate which they would not themselves have recommended.[22] The Chileans, in their presentation of their policies, played down some of their more unorthodox aspects and stressed their concern with controlling inflation; but they had at least to get acceptance for the notion that the control of inflation should be 'gradual'.

As far as criticism was concerned the main pressure in the reports, advice and negotiations of the three international agencies was on controlling public expenditure, especially

21. With the exception noted above.
22. One of the most frequently cited examples was the system of gradual adjustments of the exchange rate. The IMF would have liked once-for-all devaluation large enough to anticipate subsequent price increases.

expenditure for social purposes, and on controlling wage increases. The I M F considered that the gradual control of inflation must necessarily involve 'increasingly tighter overall financial programmes year after year'. It also felt that the policy of income redistribution must be moderated if business savings were to be promoted. In the World Bank there was concern that the public sector was 'getting too large a share of the cake'. The international agencies' solution for the problem of investment was therefore that taxation should be reduced, and they felt that the government's efforts to tax the private sector had gone too far. All three institutions were especially disturbed by the size of the government's housing programme: the A I D, it should be said, felt that the government's expenditure should be reoriented towards agriculture and other directly productive purposes; the I M F and the World Bank pressed for general limitation on the increase in public expenditure, and were alarmed that the budget deficit had not been reduced in the government's first year.

Above all, both the World Bank and the I M F came down strongly on the side of reducing the target for land reform, suggesting 20,000 or 30,000 families as more suitable targets.[23] Their main reason for doing so was that they considered the programme would be too expensive. The World Bank, indeed, on whose 1966 mission there were agricultural specialists, was of the opinion that the cost per family would be even higher than the Chileans had estimated. International officials were also concerned about the short-term effects of land reform on production; the perspective in the World Bank was 'the next four or five years'. Some still felt that higher prices were the solution for Chilean agriculture. At any rate, the decisions of the I M F and the World Bank on land reform were taken on the

23. See above, pp. 126–7.

basis of its effect on public finances and of its short-term effects on production. From both these points of view it was felt, rightly or wrongly, that land reform was undesirable, and it was therefore discouraged. Even though it was recognized at a responsible level in the World Bank that Chile's agricultural development in the long term was dependent on its basic social conflicts being resolved, it was nevertheless felt that Chile 'simply could not afford' a land-reform programme of the size proposed. As for the AID, its official attitude was fairly neutral; in the State Department it was claimed that the US 'certainly did not hold up land reform'.

For 1967 the Chilean government decided to do without an IMF stand-by and AID programme loan. This does not seem to have been because it wanted to avoid the conditions attached to them. Negotiations with the AID for a programme loan were in fact practically concluded; the Chileans told the AID they would carry out the agreed programme, and announced publicly that the loan would still be available if, for instance, copper prices fell.[24] Similarly they assured the IMF that their decision to forgo the stand-by should not be interpreted as an unwillingness to formulate financial and general economic policies within the framework of an internally consistent programme. It seems there were several reasons for deciding to do without the financial support of the two agencies. One was political; it was useful to demonstrate that the government was not wholly dependent on external support. There was also doubtless a desire to reduce this dependence in fact; Chile's heavy foreign indebtedness was an obvious limitation on its freedom of manoeuvre,[25] so long of course as it hoped for

24. The Chilean government used this option in the last quarter of 1967. See this chapter, note 17.

25. See also Philip O'Brien's forthcoming ODI study on the relationship between the AID and the Chilean authorities.

further credit in the future and was not prepared to take the drastic step of defaulting on its debts. There were in addition various practical reasons: at a time when there was a boom in foreign trade, there were strong pressures on the government to start new projects and to increase wages, especially in the copper industry, and the government wanted to put itself in a better position to resist these pressures by appealing to a patriotic desire to reduce foreign dependence. Finally of course it would have been difficult simply to put the AID loan into the reserves.

The Chilean economic authorities were not particularly bothered by the efforts of the international agencies to influence their policies. They tended to say that these efforts did no harm, and might even help in Chile's case where the authorities had a clear programme of their own which in fact they persuaded the agencies to support. They felt that in countries whose economic policies were not so clearly formulated the pressure could be more damaging. Besides, policies which the agencies supported such as reducing the budget deficit, controlling wage increases and improving the management of monetary policy, were policies with which the authorities were in any case concerned. Those policies of a more expansionist or redistributory nature, which on the whole the international agencies opposed, were carried out in spite of them. Some Chileans felt not that the international agencies approved of Chilean policies, but that, in the political situation immediately after the elections, the international agencies 'would have supported anything'; the programme was 'approved' reluctantly, but the agencies were later, on the whole, convinced by its success. As far as taxes were concerned, it was felt in one case that AID support might have had a beneficial effect in the sense that the opponents of increases in taxation could no longer expect support from the United States; the US position was described as 'a sort of green light' for taxation, and even for land reform.

It was also felt by at least one Chilean official that the discussions were useful in the sense that they enabled the Chilean authorities to clarify their ideas. Some who were concerned with excesses in certain kinds of public expenditure and in wage increases felt that their position was reinforced. The Chilean authorities also felt that the IMF and the AID were changing 'slowly and incoherently'. When asked whether international officials were capable of understanding what the Chileans were trying to do, one answer was that the quality of AID economists had gone up sharply, and they could now make a real intellectual contribution. IMF officials apparently varied; of some of those who came to Chile, the Chileans might afterwards be able to say: 'that was a good one, he understood.'

In any case, the differences between the Chilean economic authorities and the international agencies were not really fundamental. There were differences of emphasis, differences of method, and differences of understanding. But the ultimate goals were similar: both the government and the international agencies were basically in favour of financial stability, growth, a more equal distribution of income, legality and evolutionary change. The government hoped to achieve them all at once; the international agencies said Chile must choose between them, and tried to persuade the government to put stability and legality first. Whether, given even more political skill and determination, the Frei government *could* have achieved all its goals at once is doubtful. At any rate when the crunch came Chile seems to have abandoned many of its expansionist and reformist goals, and to have come down on the side of the international agencies.

BRAZIL

Before the 1964 military coup both the AID and the World Bank had ceased to lend to President Goulart's populist and leftist government. The ostensible grounds for their decisions were that Goulart's economic and social policies, which included some redistribution of income to wage-earners and the beginnings of a land reform, were creating financial 'chaos' with very high rates of inflation and the danger that Brazil might default on its debts. If inflation had continued at its early-1964 rate, it would have been between 100 and 150 per cent in 1964 as a whole. United States recognition of the new military government under General Castelo Branco was immediate, and negotiations for renewed support from the World Bank, the AID and the IMF followed. Before the end of 1964, an AID programme loan of $50 million had been provided, and further programme loans totalling $300 million were provided in 1965 and 1966. The Brazilian government, at least at the beginning, retained some of the forms of parliamentary democracy and it was claimed that it was re-establishing order and efficiency in the economy.[26] The government was also prepared to go to great lengths to maintain good relations with the United States government.[27]

Brazilian economic policies from 1964 to 1967, under the direction of Dr Roberto Campos, were in fact all that the World Bank, the IMF and the AID could desire. Campos

26. For example, the 1968 IMF *Annual Report* stated: 'About mid-1964 the Brazilian authorities initiated a broad programme of policies to reduce the rate of inflation and to lay the basis for stable economic growth' (p. 77). See also an article by a World Bank official, Irving A. Sirken, 'Fighting Inflation in Brazil: Some Tentative Lessons', in *Finance and Development*, No. 3, 1968.

27. See, for example, chapter 2, note 100.

had for years been one of the major proponents and theorists of the monetarist school of thought.[28] For his three years as Economics Minister, from the accession of the military government in 1964 to the change of president in 1967, when he was not re-appointed as Minister, he had almost total freedom of action. He was wholly backed by the military government, which was remarkably impervious to internal pressures of most varieties. He had the full agreement and co-operation of the Finance Minister, Dr Pulhoês.

Campos's policy was monetarist in its simplest and purest form. Not simple in the methods used, which were highly sophisticated, but simple in the doctrinal sense. The main concern of the Brazilian military government was to re-establish 'stability', economic and political. Stability, in the economic field, meant reducing the rate of inflation, repaying some of Brazil's debts, and restoring the reserves. In this Campos was quite successful. The rate of inflation was down to 40 per cent in 1966. Brazil paid off a considerable proportion of its debts, more, it appears, than its creditors were requiring.[29] Exports increased quite rapidly in 1965 and 1966, although this was mainly as a result of an increase of coffee exports, with possible long-term disadvantages. Brazil's net foreign reserve position improved sharply in 1965 and again improved, although to a lesser extent, in 1966. Costa e Silva, a few weeks before he succeeded Castelo Branco as President in 1967, could say in Washington that he was 'proud of Brazil's new international standing'.

But the price paid was high. The major instrument of

28. See, for instance, his contribution to *Latin American Issues, Essays and Comments*, edited by A. O. Hirschman, The Twentieth Century Fund, New York, 1961.

29. See below, p. 138.

policy was deflation. Credit was tightly controlled, and much effort was made to reduce the budgetary deficit. Wages were kept to below the rise in the cost of living. Existing industry was severely hit, and there was little new investment, in spite of selective credit and tax incentive policies. The foreign-owned motor-car industries were revived in 1965 by special diminishing tax reductions to car purchasers, but it was apparently 'more difficult' to apply measures of this sort to mass-consumption industries such as the textile industry. The inflow of foreign private investment was less than expected. By late 1966, after the money supply had been further restricted, there was a severe industrial recession, and in 1967 the recession 'deepened', as the IMF put it. It seemed that the rate of inflation might be increasing again, as a result, it was suggested, of 'cost-push' phenomena. Although figures on unemployment and on the level of real wages are inadequate, unemployment clearly increased from its already very high level, real wages declined, possibly by as much as 25 per cent in 1966,[30] and increasing numbers of those who remained in employment had their wages reduced to the statutory minimum levels. In an effort to restructure the price mechanism and to increase agricultural production, the authorities removed price controls on food, thus further aggravating conditions for the urban unemployed. Agricultural production increased substantially in 1966, but weather conditions were exceptionally good; and the main beneficiaries of increased prices were not the rural poor, but the landlords and middlemen. Imports declined heavily in 1965; they rose in 1966, but only to slightly above their 1963 level; in 1967,

30. As estimated by a member of the 1967 World Bank mission, who also calculated that minimum wages were the same, in real terms, as they had been 15 years previously, and that real wages were declining as a percentage of value added in industry.

after some import liberalization measures, they rose again, but slowly. As for social reforms and progress in education, in land tenure and in the conditions of life of the rural and urban poor, these were no part of the objectives of the military government; and social investment was minimal.[31] Finally, political repression became increasingly severe.

The international agencies, all three of which provided considerable financial support, were fairly constantly involved in discussions and negotiations with the Brazilian government. There was occasionally some disagreement, for instance, on the timing of policies, on the degree of restrictiveness required, on whether or not Brazil needed to allow an increase in imports at particular times, and so on. Sometimes, as a key State Department official put it, the international agencies 'pointed out the gaps between laudable intentions and practice'. In the AID there were a few complaints that Campos was 'more royalist than the king'. The AID was in favour of, and the IMF and the World Bank were against, Brazil using its reserves and aid to import food and consumer goods when shortages threatened to force up prices. This was particularly so in 1965. The United States was prepared to ensure that Brazilian debts were substantially rolled over and the IMF 'agreed', but Campos apparently insisted on Brazil repaying its debts at a rapid rate and accepted only a relatively minor re-scheduling. The World Bank was critical of the inadequacy of Brazilian statistics and of the authorities' knowledge and control of the economy in general. The Bank felt that the budget could and should be balanced, that

31. The policies were so unpopular that Marshal Costa e Silva had to promise to 'humanize' the government's policies when he took office, by which he meant increasing government expenditure and expanding credit for the private sector.

government expenditure, especially current expenditure, but also public investment, could be cut further, and that more credit should be made available to the private sector; it disagreed with the timing of the 1966 credit squeeze. But on the general direction and emphasis of policy, on the necessary severity of stabilization measures, on most specific questions, as was repeatedly said, there was a 'basic identity of views'.[32] The three international agencies and the Brazilian government were, as a high official in the AID put it, 'all in it together', and a study of Brazilian economic policies from 1964 to 1967 would provide a good illustration of the international agencies' ideal.

There were of course some within the international agencies who did not share this official ideal. There were also, in the AID at a high and responsible level, one or two who felt, not that the policies had been wrong, but that they had failed. Failed because the economy had stagnated: the private sector had not invested, and the expected large inflow of foreign private investment had not occurred. Failed also because in 1966, a year when the increase in the money supply had been restricted to 12–15 per cent, and effective demand was lower than in the previous year, inflation was still 40 per cent. These observations were leading to some realization, within the AID, that traditional economic instruments were not as effective as had been supposed.[33] But the main concern in the AID was with the failure of private investment. This failure was sometimes assigned to the fact that the government was military

32. At least among those responsible for official views.

33. The World Bank's 1967 Report also stated in its introduction (see below): '... it is clear now that the difficulties involved in restoring price stability in the framework of a free market mechanism are substantially greater than had been foreseen at the beginning of the stabilisation programme ...'

and investors did not have confidence in its survival. Certainly there were some AID officials who were concerned about the undemocratic nature of the Brazilian government, and about the government's excessive reliance on military strength and its failure to 'build a political base'.

Apart from this, responsible international officials seemed to share the Brazilian government's lack of concern with political and social problems. An illustration of the agencies' official attitude may perhaps be provided from the report resulting from a major World Bank mission in Brazil early in 1967. The mission included a variety of talents and opinions. But the long introduction to the final[34] version of the mission's report mentioned agriculture only in connection with price incentives and diversification from coffee exports and it did not mention educational and other social policies or unemployment at all. It stated its view of the possibilities for the Brazilian economy and concluded with the following (unshortened) list of 'requirements':

1. Very strong restraint in the current expenditure of the government and improvement in fiscal co-operation between the Treasury and the states and municipalities.

2. Very great improvement in the knowledge of – and control over – the government's own expenditure and those of its dependencies, over their borrowing and over their investment planning.

3. Sufficient austerity in the public sector's capital expenditures to permit a more adequate flow of credit to the private sector than in the past, without excessive overall credit expansion.

4. Effective action to eliminate the production and accumulation of unsaleable coffee.

5. Continued readiness to adjust the exchange rate to the

34. And therefore least secret: see p. 72.

degree needed to keep Brazilian production competitive with the rest of the world.

6. Continued willingness of the authorities to rationalize and liberalize restrictions on imports.

7. Pressing forward with the policy of letting prices be determined by the market mechanism rather than by administrative fiat.

8. Above all else, that a sense of continuity and stability pervade the economy, so that the private sector is convinced that the framework for investment decisions – taxation, price determination, exchange control, property rights, etc. – will not be modified lightly and without due process of law.

There were many Brazilians, in official or semi-official positions, who resented the activities of the international agencies. Some resented the time spent by a few responsible and overworked Brazilian officials in answering their questions. Some felt that the concentration, by the World Bank in particular, on the collection of statistics, was beside the point; it was suggested for instance that World Bank officials would believe that unemployment existed only if there were figures to say so and were oblivious to the sight of people sleeping in the street. Much of the serious criticism of the international agencies came from those who were also critical of Campos's policies, especially those who believed that it would have been possible to have expansionist policies and pay more attention to social problems, with the same rate of inflation or even a lower one.

There were also some Brazilians, again officials or established intellectuals, who felt that, on balance, the move by international agencies towards more concern with general policies was a useful one. This was not necessarily the view only of those whose policies the international agencies were supporting. There were also some who felt that a broadening of the international agencies' concern must mean that they would begin to pay more attention to the long term. They hoped the international agencies would, eventually, learn. It was said that Brazilian officials negotiating on the scheme for Supplementary Financial Measures[35] had accepted the principle of the scheme as inevitable. If the governments of developing countries were to get financial support, they would have to agree to agency policies. The Brazilians were concentrating on trying to ensure that the policies would be good policies; that international civil servants were more competent, had a wider understanding of political and social problems and were more prepared to accept that developing countries had to move fast. There was much agreement among Brazilian officials that the international agencies, to varying degrees, made the mistake of believing that financial problems could be solved in isolation and also that they had an excessively narrow and quantitative view of reality.

The significance of the international agencies' support for the Brazilian government's policies from 1964 to 1967 was not so much that they affected these policies as that they were the sort of policies of which they approved. The policies were Campos's. Claims by the international agencies that they strengthened his resolve are rather dubious. At most, they may have strengthened his position within the government, for example by formally embodying his policies in loan agreements. This was effective in Brazil's case, in a way that it might not be elsewhere, because of the Castelo Branco Government's particular concern with pleasing its international creditors.

35. See above, pp. 54–6.

PERU

Peru was one of the first Latin-American countries in which the IMF was involved, and from 1954 it had a fairly continuous and close relationship with the Fund. Its economic situation in the early 1960s, after a stabilization programme in 1959, was sometimes held to prove the validity of IMF policies. In this period Peru had rapid growth, financial stability, no balance of payments problems, almost no exchange or import controls and a very low level of government expenditure and revenues. The World Bank and the AID were little involved.

But Peru's combination of growth and financial stability was somewhat illusory. The growth started from a low base and was mainly the result of foreign private investment; it was therefore confined to Lima and one or two other coastal areas. Large areas of the country, particularly the highly populated *sierra* or mountain areas, were barely touched. Their social and material situation, partly as a result of an extremely inequitable system of land tenure, was desperate. There was heavy migration to slums in coastal cities. Even from the point of view of further economic growth, Peru probably needed to expand its internal market. As for the balance of payments, imports were low partly because the consuming population was small. Above all, Peru was lucky with the prices and markets for its exports, especially fishmeal. But by the mid-1960s the boom in fishmeal exports was coming to an end, and Peru was having difficulties with its exports of sugar and cotton.[36]

36. For an analysis of the effects of the 1959 stabilization programme in Peru, concluding that its apparent success was to be ascribed mainly to favourable export circumstances not influenced by Peruvian policies,

In 1963 the Belaúnde government came into office. One of its major policies was to open up the interior of Peru and integrate '*los olvidados*' – the forgotten people – into the economy. It began spending. Since it was in a hurry it spent, no doubt, in rather a haphazard way. Belaúnde[37] had his own rather particular vision, and his vision tended to express itself in terms of physical achievements: the Mantaro dam project, projects for opening up new agricultural lands, major irrigation works in the coastal desert, roads in the interior, above all the *carretera marginal*, a great road along the potentially fertile jungle-covered eastern slopes of the Andes. In addition some interesting experiments were started in the *sierra*, particularly the programme of '*cooperación popular*' and efforts to revive some of the Indian communal systems of agriculture (although the problem of land tenure was barely touched). There was also a large housing programme. When the institutions capable of providing long-term finance for such projects demanded a cautious appraisal of their usefulness, Belaúnde lost patience; Columbus, he said, would never have discovered America if he had waited for the results of feasibility studies. Peru, partly because of its past stability and liberal economic policies, was able to borrow freely in New York and Europe and contracted large amounts of short-term high-interest debt. Some of the contractors, as an additional inducement, provided funds, on equally bad terms, which constituted almost a parallel budget.

The Belaúnde government was moreover unable, mainly because of the intransigence of Congress, partly perhaps because of a lack of concern and political will, to increase

see Rosemary Thorp, 'Inflation and Orthodox Economic Policy in Peru', *Bulletin of the Oxford Institute of Economics and Statistics*, August 1967.

37. Who was an architect by training.

its revenues from taxation. In the 1960s tax revenues were declining as a proportion of national income. The Belaúnde government did not have a majority in Congress and it owed its position partly to the support of the military. The main political platform of the opposition parties, including the once supposedly revolutionary Apra, was '*no más impuestos*': no more taxes. As a result of all this, there were increasing budgetary deficits. By the beginning of 1967 Peru's reserves were running out and there was talk of crisis and devaluation.[38] The international agencies were by now, of course, concerned.

The World Bank and the AID, at any rate at the beginning of the Belaúnde government's period in office, were in favour of the plans to expand public investment. A 1965 World Bank mission gave its blessing to such an expansion; it was acknowledged that development in Peru had been concentrated in a very small area and even that private enterprise would not provide economic opportunities for the people of the *sierra*. As a mark of its approval of Peru's new policies the Bank indeed set up a consultative group which met for the first time in 1966. The Bank concentrated on trying to improve the Peruvian government's planning of its investment and on persuading it to consolidate and maintain what it had begun. The Bank's negotiations for project loans were, as usual, for roads, the railway, power and some large irrigation projects on the coast. The AID and the IADB were also involved in the financing of roads. The three agencies tried to work together to agree on priorities, and held discussions *à quatre* with the Peruvians during which the idea of the *carretera marginal* was generally approved. The IADB also had some rather more adventurous projects in the *sierra*, where it suppor-

38. Devaluation was generally regarded as a political humiliation. It did in fact occur in September 1967.

ted some of the government's experiments in agriculture.

Possibly the most controversial aspect of the international agencies' activities in the first years of the Belaúnde government was their reluctance to agree to finance the government's projects without long and careful appraisal. Project financing is outside the scope of this study. But the cautiousness of the international agencies did have its effect on Peru's general policies, since it is sometimes argued that Peru was 'driven to Wall Street' by it, and the size of the short-term debt thus contracted was one of the causes of the crisis in 1967. It might have been possible for the World Bank, in particular, to show more sympathy with the sense of urgency of the Belaúnde government. There was, in this sense, some conflict between the World Bank's concern with the economy as a whole and its concern with the direct financial return of particular projects. The Projects Department in the Bank is, and was designed to be, a bottleneck holding up decisions. There is little doubt that its procedures are unwieldy. In Peru's case it can be argued that the Projects Department took a narrow view even at the level of deciding between projects. For instance the Bank decided that it would be prepared to finance an irrigation project which was likely to produce fairly high financial returns at Olmos but not a financially less viable project near Arequipa. It was not prepared to accept the Peruvian government's view that priorities should be determined by the fact that the Arequipa area, unlike Olmos, suffered from political and social strains and strong population pressure. The Bank's argument that 'people can be moved' is not convincing; if the Arequipa project, as proposed by the Peruvians, was unsatisfactory, it might have been possible to think of an alternative in the same area. On the other hand it is obviously difficult to weigh the need to ensure that projects are viable against the need for rapidity in decision;

it seems that in the case of the Mantaro dam project, for instance, the Peruvian government might have done better, even from the point of view of speed, to accept World Bank advice in dealing with contractors (including British contractors). The IADB, which makes a commitment to lend and negotiates conditions afterwards, was not notably more successful in shortening the time spent in negotiation.

Apart from the question of project negotiations, the World Bank and the AID, as well as the IMF, were of course by 1967 involved in questions of general policy. The IMF, which had a resident representative advising the central bank, felt that devaluation could be avoided if the budgetary deficit was controlled. The World Bank felt that devaluation was necessary, but was not prepared to press for it. As far as the budgetary deficit was concerned, there was agreement that the main problem was the failure to increase tax revenues. There was some concern about the increase in the government's current expenditures, particularly those earmarked for social purposes, and about the direction of public investment; there was also some suggestion that a wage freeze was necessary. But the international agencies' view was that the general level of public investment was excessive only if nothing was done about public revenues.

The World Bank sent a number of missions to Peru at the end of 1966 and beginning of 1967. It became clear that there was little hope of the Bank calling another meeting of the consultative group until Peru had solved its fiscal problems; it was also conceivable that the Bank would consider holding up loan commitments. Despite some doubts which it shared with others as to whether it was the 'right package', the Bank had put its weight behind a set of specific proposals for increasing tax revenues made by an OAS mission. Some suspected the Bank of wanting an increase in petrol taxes in order to help the British-owned railway company which was in danger of defaulting on a World Bank loan. Others criticized the Bank for lack of firmness and in particular for failing to object when the army allocated most of the proceeds of new import tariffs to itself. But with the general objective of more taxation nobody but the Peruvian oligarchs could disagree.

The AID mission in Peru was also engaged in trying to persuade the Peruvian government of the seriousness of the fiscal situation and the accumulation of short-term debt. The idea of a programme loan with conditions was being discussed. There were some in the AID mission who felt that programme loans were an instrument that needed great care in manipulation, and that direct threats to cut aid if certain things were not done were likely to be counter-productive. But, whatever the mission may have felt about it, a small programme loan was discussed in the spring of 1967 and finally rejected by Peru.

No doubt the programme loan would have had as a condition that the Peruvian government should be successful in increasing tax revenues. But the main reason for the refusal of the loan was that it had a number of other conditions which were purely and simply intended to promote US interests. There were three main conditions: Peru was asked to buy US planes, subsonic and more expensive, instead of French supersonic Mirages; to allow US ships to fish within a 200-mile limit in which Peru was trying to control fishing in the off-season in order to preserve stocks; and not to allow the Peruvian state oil company to take over an oil-field whose ownership had long been disputed with the IPC, the US oil company in Peru.

These conditions to an offer of a programme loan to Peru were part of a long series of United States efforts to get its interests looked after in Peru. The US had already on earlier occasions threatened to cut off aid in connection with Peru's treatment of the oil company and of its fishing-boats. At other times the US-owned Lima telephone company (I T & T) entered the discussions. On a later occasion, when the Peruvian government attempted to give the new Peruvian shipping line some minor preferential treatment over the US Grace Shipping Line, the State Department threatened to close US markets to Peruvian exports of sugar and other commodities. In all this the disproportion between the nature of the interests concerned – vital to Peru, secondary to the United States – tends to be rather flagrant.[39] And the question of the Peruvian government raising taxes, whether or not this is considered to be a legitimate concern for the United States, inevitably gets rather lost.

39. The pressures culminated in a military take-over at the end of 1968. The new military government nationalized the disputed IPC interests, and as a result is threatened with the application of the Hickenlooper Amendment involving loss of US aid and, according to some interpretations, of Peru's sugar quota in the United States market. US aid has been run down to virtually nil, and the question of Peru's sugar quota has been shelved, for the moment, which was possible partly because of a bad Peruvian harvest in 1968. The US position is weakened by the fact that there is no important or vocal section of the Peruvian population which is opposed to the government's nationalization policies, and by the fact that there were, at any rate in the early stages of the military government, no forces to the right of the present military junta on internal affairs.

Chapter 4

COMMENTS AND CONCLUSIONS[1]

THE NATURE OF THE PROCESS OF LEVERAGE

THE involvement of the international agencies in general economic policies is not, as is sometimes supposed, a process in which officials of the agencies and of the government concerned sit down together and discuss, with open minds, the best solutions to the government's particular problems. Nor is the agencies' role limited, as it is sometimes suggested that it should be, to making suggestions and pointing out mistakes, without taking advantage of the fact that they have power over the allocation of financial resources.

The process is rather one in which the international agencies attempt to ensure that policies on which they themselves have decided are adopted by the governments hoping to receive aid. If governments are, in any case, pursuing such policies, the international agencies will probably support them and try to contribute to the success of the policies. If they are not, the international agencies are concerned, more or less actively, to ensure that they change; negotiations may lead to compromise, to some modification in the agencies' demands, but not to change in their general pattern and emphasis. On occasion the international agencies have demanded, as a condition of their support, the adoption of specific policies with little prior consultation

1. This chapter is based on the evidence provided in chapters 2 and 3, but not exclusively so; it is the result of discussion and reading about the issues in general, which was of course not confined to the four countries discussed in chapter 3.

with the government concerned. Governments with clearly defined economic policies may, provided the policies are within a general framework acceptable to the agencies, be able to negotiate the acceptance of their own policies and some concessions by the agencies. But the nature and direction of the agencies' demands is predictable. Latin-American governments are not in any doubt as to the kind of policies they need to pursue in order to get the support of the IMF and hence, as has been shown, of the AID and the World Bank.

It is sometimes maintained that the international agencies confine themselves to recommendations of a technical nature, and avoid ideological issues. Their concentration on fiscal and monetary matters has on occasion been justified on these grounds. But, as will be argued later, such concentration not only implies neglect of other problems, but frequently conflicts with their solution. No issues are purely technical. The agencies' policies, when they are adopted, have profound implications for the nature and priorities of society, and are based on values and assumptions in a way which is the more insidious for not always being made explicit. In the agencies' reports, and even less in their demands, little attempt is made to discuss the implications of different policy measures or to suggest alternative methods, still less alternative ends. The claims of objectivity and of having 'no axe to grind', made especially by the World Bank, are misleading, in so far as they are believed.

The agencies' policies presuppose a liberal form of economic organization and adherence to international rules as defined in the West. They are based on the acceptance and upholding of the existing international and national framework of the capitalist world: as chapter 2 tried to show, the international agencies cannot accept changes in developing countries which might endanger existing patterns of international trade, foreign private investment, the regular servicing and repayment of debts, and other more or less general concerns of the capitalist developed or creditor countries. There is a strong emphasis in the agencies' policies and demands on the principles of free enterprise, on reliance on market mechanisms, and on the respect of private property, domestic and especially foreign. The need for change is, to some extent, acknowledged; but the first priority is stability. Right-wing and military dictatorships with little or no concern for development, in the sense of raising the standards of living of all sections of the community, are acceptable, and indeed typical, recipients of aid so long as they offer the prospect of economic and financial stability. It may be said that the international agencies are merely trying to ensure the smooth functioning of a system which they themselves are powerless to change, and that in any case it is undesirable that it should change. But, at any rate, it should not be claimed that their judgements are value-free, or that their attitudes are neutral.

Supposing that partiality of this variety is accepted as desirable, some subsidiary questions arise. The first is whether the international agencies' economic analysis is, or can be, adequate. It is possible to point to mistakes and inconsistencies in agency reports, and to demands which fail to produce the results expected of them, even within the given set of assumptions. The economic sophistication of members of agency missions is sometimes less than that of the government officials they are dealing with; in this case the justification for their pressure is presumably that the pressure is towards certain general objectives, not that it contributes specifically to the effectiveness of government policies. It is not altogether clear whether such failings could be remedied by improvements in the staff and methods of international agencies, or whether they are inherent in a system in which external agencies attempt to understand and pronounce upon the problems of countries with which they are relatively unfamiliar. There is the additional problem that few economic policies can be effective in isolation; they require the full commitment and understanding of the governments expected to implement them. It may be, as has frequently been argued, that the expertise of foreigners is more likely to be useful in well-defined sectors than on more general economic issues.

Second, there is the question of the extent to which leverage is effective in what it is trying to achieve. Developed countries have other means, more powerful than aid, of inducing developing countries not to disrupt existing relationships. The attempt to use aid to promote specific changes in policies may be counter-productive. In some cases it has merely led to confusion, crisis and delay. In many others it has simply meant no aid, or less aid while the government continued as before, sometimes because the amounts offered were too small for it to be worth the government's while to change its policies in order to get them. The efforts of the international agencies to secure the adoption of particular policies may in fact have the opposite effect, increasing governments' resistance to the policies on the grounds that adopting them would be a demonstration of subservience, or ensuring that, supposing the government is forced to adopt them, it does so with such unwillingness that the necessary complementary actions are not taken and the policies can be shown to fail. It may be that leverage only appears to be 'effective', in the sense that the agencies' policies are adopted in a fairly consistent and systematic manner, in countries whose government would have pursued these or similar policies in any case; the actual result is then simply that these governments are rewarded with larger sums of aid. It has been argued, even by those who agree with the general objectives of the international agencies, that it is better to abandon the complications of influencing general economic policies in order to maintain a flow of resources, possibly for projects and sectors in which the agencies' advice can be useful.[2]

EFFECTS OF THE INTERNATIONAL AGENCIES POLICIES IN LATIN AMERICA

But the above are, as has been said, subsidiary questions. The crucial issue is whether the present systems of economic and social organization in Latin America, based on private enterprise, a respect for property however unequally distributed, and economic and political dependence on the United States, are capable of providing real improvements in the conditions of life of the mass of the people. The policies of the international agencies imply that they are, or that such improvement is unnecessary, or secondary to other considerations, or simply that the United States, supported by the major financial agencies, is determined to preserve the existing situation for as long as possible.

Whatever the reasons, the international agencies are in

2. For a fuller discussion of such questions, concluding that 'the explicit conditioning of aid on changes in policies of the recipient countries should be avoided' and 'elaborate arrangements should be made to divorce the exchange of opinions about suitable economic policies from the actual aid-giving process', see Albert O. Hirschman, 'Foreign Aid – A Critique and a Proposal', in A. O. Hirschman (ed.), *Latin American Issues, Essays and Comments*, The Twentieth Century Fund, New York, 1961. See also John White, *Pledged to Development*, ODI, 1967; and Andrzej Krassowski, *The Aid Relationship*, ODI, 1968.

fact pursuing policies which distract attention from, and frequently conflict with, action to improve the conditions of life of the majority of Latin Americans. As has been shown in chapters 2 and 3, they have concentrated on financial and monetary issues, and in particular on efforts to achieve or maintain financial and monetary stability. But their stabilization programmes have rarely been successful, even in their own terms; that is, prices have continued to rise, and the private sector has not made the response expected of it. The more common result is recession and political crisis so that the government, or its successor, is forced to abandon the stabilization programme. The international agencies, while modifying some aspects of their policies, have continued to maintain that such programmes could be successful if they were pursued with more resolution and persistence, and that financial and monetary stabilization is an essential precondition of, for example, growth, a redistribution of income, and increases in social expenditures, in so far as the latter are considered desirable objectives. Growth in particular is expected to be a consequence of stabilization programmes, even sometimes a direct consequence, in the sense that it is expected to come about more or less automatically once correct fiscal and monetary policies have restored price equilibrium disturbed by previous government action. In any case, objectives other than stabilization have been sacrificed with a certain amount of equanimity pending the achievement of stabilization; and since stabilization is rarely achieved, governments wishing to pursue other objectives must usually do so without the support, or without the full support, of the international agencies.

With few exceptions, stabilization programmes supported by the international agencies have resulted in low or zero rates of growth, and low or negative rates of *per capita* growth, during the period when stabilization was attempted.[3] It is true that there is now more concern that

3. Peru, in the early 1960s, has been claimed as an exception; but the success ended when fishmeal prices weakened and the government began spending; see chapter 3, section on Peru; see also Rosemary Thorp, 'Inflation and Orthodox Economic Policy in Peru', *Bulletin of the Oxford Institute of Economics and Statistics*, August 1967. The latest stabilization programme in Argentina, which had some new features, showed signs of being more successful, in the short run, than previous ones, partly as a result of a large inflow of foreign private investment; but it is doubtful whether the improvement could have been maintained, once the new foreign investment had resulted in higher remittances abroad of profits and interest; in any case the programme intensified already acute political and social tensions and contributed to the major political crisis which began in June 1969 and still continues, and which of course led to modification of the government's programme and renewed economic crisis. On Brazil, see chapter 3, section on Brazil. In Venezuela and Mexico, the two Latin-American countries which have had long periods of growth and financial stability, this achievement is sometimes ascribed to the pursuit of policies of the sort favoured by the international agencies; but exceptional factors – in Venezuela oil, and in Mexico tourism and the 1920 revolution – are probably of greater importance. There are a number of published descriptions and criticisms of stabilization programmes and their effects. See for example I. Eshag and R. Thorp, 'Economic and Social Consequences of Orthodox Policies in Argentina in the Post-War Years', *Bulletin of the Oxford Institute of Economics and Statistics*, February 1965; O. Braun and L. Joy, 'A Model of Economic Stagnation – A Case Study of Argentina', *Economic Journal*, December 1968; Carlos Diaz-Alejandro, *Exchange-Rate Devaluation in a Semi-Industrialized Country: the Experience of Argentina, 1955–1961*, Massachusetts Institute of Technology Press, 1966; Francis Masson and James Theberge, 'External Capital Requirements and Economic Development. The Case of Argentina', *Journal of the Royal Statistical Society*, Volume 130, Part 3, 1967; 'Argentina and the IMF: possibilities of constructive co-operation', *Review of the River Plate*, February 1966, text of an IMF Report and of a letter to the Managing Director of the IMF from the Argentine Minister of the Economy; George Jackson Eder, *Inflation and Development in Latin America – A Case History of Inflation and Stabilisation in Bolivia*, Michigan University Press, 1968; A. O. Hirschman,

stabilization programmes should not induce stagnation. The international agencies seem prepared to accept that stabilization should be achieved 'gradually'. Meanwhile they are not averse to some attention being paid to increasing government revenues, to public investment policies, to export diversification, to the provision of certain incentives for agricultural production, and especially to the encouragement of private investment. They show signs of accepting some arguments about the need for productive investment on the grounds that inflation is caused partly by problems of supply. Increases in aid may themselves contribute to investment and growth.[4] But, at least as far as positive measures are concerned, the international agencies' concern with growth remains secondary to their concern with stabilization. Their main reason for pressing for increases in government revenues arises from their desire to reduce government deficits, 'because we can't stop governments spending', as an IMF official put it. As far as the private sector is concerned, the effects of the programmes are mixed. The hopes for increased private investment depend largely on the somewhat unlikely hypothesis that the private sector will have confidence in the final outcome of the

Journeys Towards Progress, Anchor Books, Doubleday & Co., Inc., New York, 1965; Juan Vásquez Noyola, 'El Desarrollo Económico y la Inflación en México y en otros países Latino-Americanos', *Investigación Económica*, octubre/diciembre 1956; Leopoldo Solis, 'Inflación, Estabilidad y Desarrollo: el Caso de México', *El Trimestre Económico*, julio/septiembre 1968; Couriel and Lichtensztejn, *El F.M.I. y la Crisis Económica Nacional*, Montevideo, 1968, pp. 91–139; Norman Macraed, 'No Christ on the Andes, An Economic Survey of Latin America', published as a supplement to the *Economist*, 25 September 1965 (on Argentina, Brazil and Mexico). See also chapter 2, note 23.

4. But see Keith Griffin, paper presented to a conference at the African Centre (mimeographed), in which he argues, partly on the basis of historical correlations, that higher levels of aid tend to result in lower levels of savings and total investment in Latin America.

stabilization programme and will invest with a renewed feeling of certainty; on the greater availability of spare parts and raw materials to be achieved by import liberalization measures, although deflation and devaluation may reduce the total level of imports; and, for foreign firms, on the greater likelihood that they will be able to repatriate their profits. The adverse effects of stabilization programmes are immediate and tangible: demand and the availability of credit are reduced; import liberalization, if its effects are not balanced by devaluation, reduces protection from foreign manufactured goods; devaluation and the removal of price controls increase costs; devaluation may also redistribute income in favour of the rich, thus possibly further reducing demand.[5] As for measures to encourage agricultural production, these have on the whole been limited to price incentives and occasionally the provision of credit, in so far as general credit restrictions allow, and their effect so far has been small. Stabilization programmes still tend to have generally depressive effects on production and growth.

They have other effects about which the international agencies show fewer signs of concern. Action to reverse the deterioration in standards of living and the increasing underemployment in many rural areas, to reduce the massive flow of people into urban slums, and to improve social conditions, is postponed and neglected. Such growth as does occur, especially when it is limited to the private sector, tends to be concentrated in the cities. The emphasis on reducing budget deficits means that a very common demand is that government spending should be limited or cut. This is particularly true for programmes considered to be of a 'non-productive' or social nature: for example

5. See Carlos Diaz-Alejandro, *Exchange-Rate Devaluation in a Semi-Industrialized Country: the Experience of Argentina, 1955–1961*, Massachusetts Institute of Technology Press, 1966.

expenditures on social services, salaries and wages, housing, health, education and land reform. It is true that the importance of education and agriculture has been stressed in the public pronouncements of the AID and, more recently, of the World Bank. But, in so far as concern is shown for these sectors, the emphasis is on the contribution they can make to increased output and, in the case of agriculture, to stabilization, through increasing the supply of food.[6] In any case they are most unlikely to be the subject of specific 'performance' conditions, and the expenditures permitted, or conceivably encouraged, for example by the AID, are limited and partial.

In particular the question of agriculture, on the rather rare occasions when it arises, is seldom discussed in relation to the general improvement of conditions in rural areas. The desirability of land reform, for example, is in practice evaluated in terms of its effect on agricultural production and on public finances. Land-reform programmes conducted by reformist governments obviously involve some charge on the latter. Since the international agencies are now convinced that land reform is also likely, in the short-term, to have a negative effect on production, except in a few cases of very badly utilized land, they tend actually to discourage it.[7] Arguments that land reform is an essential prerequisite of long-term development carry little weight, since the international agencies are mainly concerned with short-term stability. The international agencies' interest in agriculture is usually confined, as has been said, to the removal of price controls, the diversification of agricultural exports and possibly the provision of credit. Aid-financed projects in agriculture are mainly large highly-mechanized commercial farms, often producing livestock. This may or

6. See below, pp. 163-4.
7. See for instance chapter 3, section on Chile.

may not be the quickest way of increasing agricultural production and agricultural exports. But Latin-American peasants benefit little, if at all, from policy measures of this sort. Systems of land tenure are such that agricultural credit, the benefits of higher prices and higher profits, often go to middlemen or to large landlords, who may in any case not be interested in increasing the productivity of the land. On balance the poor, especially of course the urban poor, are likely to suffer rather than benefit from higher prices for food.

Stabilization programmes also tend to reduce employment, in both the public and the private sectors. In the private sector some existing industries are forced to lay off workers, and there is generally, as has been said, a failure to encourage new industries. In the public sector, the international agencies, especially the World Bank, sometimes press for a reduction in employment, without considering the possibility of alternative employment.[8] Most Latin-American countries already suffer acutely from unemployment and underemployment, with high rates of population increase, with heavy migration from rural areas to cities, with the problems aggravated by increases in automation and mechanization, and frequently with large numbers of landless and underemployed peasants in rural areas. Recent studies, by ECLA and the IADB in particular, have shown that this situation is getting worse, and in several

8. Possibly the most important case is in Argentina, where the World Bank extracted a promise from the military government to reduce employment in the railways by 70,000 people; one of the most senior World Bank officials concerned had no views on alternative employment for them, except that they 'could always go "back" (*sic*) to rural areas' (from which few of them have come since the 1940s; and in any case many of the railway employees are 'white-collar' workers, not easy to integrate into agriculture, where employment opportunities are being reduced by mechanization).

countries the numbers of people employed in industry, for example, are declining. Unemployment is a problem which urgently needs to be solved, not aggravated. Yet the international agencies are prepared to add to existing unemployment for the sake of 'stability'.

The international agencies' policies thus perpetuate, and sometimes increase, the existing severe inequalities in the distribution of income and power in Latin-American countries. They do so not only by discouraging and postponing investment, exerting at times a depressive influence on production, and demanding limitations in government expenditure, especially of a social nature, but also in more direct ways. The policies, as has been said, may increase unemployment. Frequently the removal of price controls, on food in particular, is demanded. In addition, a typical objective is to ensure that nominal wages do not increase, or that increases are limited, usually to below the rise in the cost of living;[9] although it is true that some wage-earners are privileged in relation to some peasants and to the unemployed or semi-employed, they are not privileged in relation to land-owners, businessmen and politicians, none of whom are made to suffer materially from the international agencies' policies. Partial exception to these anti-egalitarian tendencies is the demand for increases in government revenues. But frequently the international agencies merely press for increases in indirect taxes, or in the rates charged for public utilities, many of which weigh most heavily on the poorer sectors of the population; and the agencies have also been known to express the opinion that a redistribution of income through taxation has gone too far, on the grounds that the savings of the rich will be affected.[10]

The international agencies have, to put it crudely, a

9. See for example chapter 3, section on Brazil, pp. 136-7.
10. See for example chapter 3, section on Chile, p. 131.

hierarchy of concerns. First, stability. Second, growth, which is often equated with 'development'. Third, a number of questions whose importance officials are prepared to acknowledge, in particular in terms of their possible contribution to stability or output, but which may be dismissed as social rather than economic questions, and which in any case, when it comes to practical policy, are virtually disregarded: the distribution of income, employment, health, education, even agriculture, and in general the material and social conditions of the rural and urban poor. Of course it is argued that stability is a precondition of growth, and that growth is a precondition of the rest; that problems of financial and monetary instability are so urgent and immediate that they must be attended to first; and so on. But how much longer do the international agencies expect Latin-American governments to be able to pursue, to the exclusion of most other things, the elusive goal of 'stability'?

ALTERNATIVE POLICIES IN LATIN AMERICA

(i) *Reforms*

Alternatives, of a sort which do not fundamentally disrupt the *status quo*, and which do not necessarily involve severance of relations with the industrial countries and the international agencies, have been tried or proposed on a number of occasions.

One alternative is growth with inflation, as for example in Brazil under Kubitschek, and with some redistribution, as in Brazil under Goulart before the 1964 military coup. The international agencies believe that this creates chaos, that growth cannot be sustained under these conditions, and that inflation, in any case, harms the poor if anything more than the rich, who have ways of getting round it. It is also suggested that periodic bouts of deflation of the IMF variety are necessary simply to prevent inflation from developing into hyper-inflation. At any rate, those who now believe that there are alternative feasible policies for Latin America, of a reformist and expansionist nature, usually argue that it is possible to have more growth, a redistribution of income in a progressive direction, and less inflation, *simultaneously*, indeed that these three objectives are not alternatives of one another, but conditions. Their argument rests on the view that it is not possible to control inflation merely by restricting demand, and that its underlying causes, as opposed to its symptoms, are primarily bottlenecks in supply, especially in food and in imports. Therefore inflation cannot be cured without growth and, it is generally added, without some redistribution of income in favour of the poor, which will change the pattern of demand, and some important 'structural' changes, especially in the system of land tenure. It is further argued that Latin-American problems can to a considerable extent be traced to balance of payments difficulties, and that these in turn are caused primarily by the deterioration in primary producers' terms of trade during the 1950s, a deterioration which is likely to continue in the future; therefore efforts are made to persuade[11] industrialized countries to change their trading policies; otherwise, it is maintained, stability and growth in Latin America will be hard to achieve.

This, very roughly, is the position of the now famous school of 'structuralists'.[12] Structuralist ideas were evolved

11. For example, through the United Nations Conference on Trade and Development (UNCTAD).

12. Structuralists sometimes also argue that stabilization programmes of the purely deflationary variety are in any case impossible to implement for political reasons.

mainly by Latin Americans in ECLA,[13] in opposition to the generally accepted orthodoxy of the international agencies and their followers, which came to be known as 'monetarist'. There has been some reconciliation of the two schools of thought, and structuralist ideas have had some influence on the international agencies.[14] As has been said, the international agencies are rather more concerned than they used to be with problems of supply, with the revenue side of the budget, and with agricultural production; they seem, on the whole, prepared to accept the idea of 'gradual' stabilization. But they are not interested in the structuralists' arguments on income distribution and the need for structural reform. There remains considerable unwillingness to discuss structuralist ideas seriously, or to depart from the agencies' basic emphasis on the limitation of demand in Latin-American countries.

Moreover, the international agencies have shown no particular interest in the structuralist theses on the balance of payments difficulties of Latin-American countries, and the responsibility of developed countries for these difficulties. Of course it is not surprising that the changes most effectively pressed for are in the weaker, or dependent, countries. The power of the international agencies to influence the trading policies of developed countries is little greater than that of Latin Americans. They can do little more than exhort. The World Bank and the IMF are now, at the request of UNCTAD, studying the problems of primary producers; they have drawn attention to the

13. Economic Commission for Latin America, or CEPAL. There is a large structuralist literature: see chapter 2, note 24.

14. A confrontation of the two schools of thought took place at a conference in Rio de Janeiro in 1963, a report of which was published in *Inflation and Growth in Latin America*, edited by W. Baer and I. Kerstenetsky, published by Irwin for the Economic Growth Center at Yale University.

seriousness of developing countries' debt problems, and they have argued for increased aid. On the other hand, officials in high positions in international agencies continue to maintain that Latin-American problems can be ascribed to their governments' mismanagement, in particular of fiscal and monetary affairs. They have produced no fundamental criticism or evaluation of the effects of the international trading and monetary system on developing countries, concentrating instead on upholding this system; they are apparently not preoccupied by the injustices of a partial free-market system in a world of unequal economic powers; and the theory of a long-term decline in the terms of trade for primary commodity producers is, rightly or wrongly, rejected.

Among most officials in the international agencies there is a similar unwillingness, reflected in their actual policies, to take seriously other suggestions for reforms and other doubts about the efficacy and universal validity of economic instruments which were evolved in, and for, the United States, Britain and a few other industrialized countries.[15] The international agencies are in effect trying to apply in Latin America a rather classical and mechanistic version of

15. See, for example, the proceedings of the Manchester Conference on Teaching Economic Development 1964 (details, chapter 1, note 15), especially paper by Dudley Seers, 'The Limitations of the Special Case'; Lauchlin Currie, *Accelerating Development, the Necessity and the Means*, McGraw-Hill, 1966. It is true that Seers' paper is referred to by Andrew S. Kamarck, who also says: 'In my view, there is no standard pattern, no one royal road to development. Each country must make its own way. ... What must *not* be done is to take an actual or mental model that has been worked out for a developed country, apply it to the developing country and, where the developing country does not fit, prescribe the changes that will make it conform to the model' (*Some Aspects of the Economic Philosophy of the World Bank*, World Bank, September 1968). But this is nevertheless quite a good description of the World Bank's current approach.

economic theories (on, for example, the means of maintaining a balanced economy through adjustments in the general level of demand) which are already partly discredited even in the apparently more propitious circumstances of, say, Britain. These theories largely fail to take account of some of the major characteristics of Latin America and indeed of most less-developed countries: for instance, the concentration of growth in a few small areas, the extremely unequal distribution of income, the existence of a great deal of unemployment, the difficulty of promoting agricultural changes when people are on the edge of subsistence, the very high rate of population increase, the dominance of foreign firms, the high dependence of the economy on the export sector, and in general the difficulty of regarding developing countries as homogeneous units, able to regulate their problems independently of external influences. Other institutions and people – Latin-American governments and academics, ECLA, even the Inter-American Development Bank – show signs of concern with questions such as how to absorb the increase in population, the value of labour-intensive techniques, the means of promoting rural change, the problems of urban '*marginalidad*', and above all the increases in unemployment and the continuation, in some cases the aggravation, of severe inequalities in the distribution of income. But on the whole it is quite complacently assumed that Latin-American countries will merely repeat the experiences of the United States and other industrialized countries. Meanwhile Latin America's major problems of hunger, disease and poverty are not faced, let alone resolved.

The question is whether they *can* be resolved, given acceptance of the existing internal and external institutional framework and economic relationships. Given such acceptance, it is arguable that the general pattern of the agencies' policies, in their attempt to preserve the system and ensure its stability, could not be much improved; and that the sacrifices involved, for those whom the system is not designed to benefit, are unavoidable.

The history of 'reformist' governments – such as the governments of Chile, Colombia and Peru in the period covered by this study – whose leaders appeared to be aware of the urgency and seriousness of the problems and willing to do something about them, has not been particularly successful either. Heroic efforts are required to get any measures of reform through congress. Parliaments tend to represent, at best, sectional interests, when they are not simply instruments for protecting the privileges of landlords and preventing the raising of taxes. Reforms are passed, in an adulterated form, after two or three years of battle and occasionally the artificial creation of crises. The implementation of such reforms is slow and partial, partly for financial reasons; modest targets are revised downwards when governments find they cannot 'afford' reform. Governments seem unable to raise or save money in places where it hurts anybody but those whose interests are inadequately represented in the present power-structure – generally the peasants and the urban unemployed. Attempts to spend money in spite of this inability lead to financial crises, which provide pretexts for military take-overs, and lead to the re-imposition of stabilization measures of the traditional variety. Such governments are probably pursuing incompatible goals in attempting both to preserve the special advantages and privileges of the rich, whom they represent, and to reduce social tensions by attempting to alleviate the conditions of the poor.

The great inequalities of income, which show little sign of changing and in some cases are increasing, mean that investments are made to satisfy a distorted pattern of demand. Some of the relatively subtle ways in which present economic policies distract attention from basic problems, or conflict with their solution, have been mentioned. There are other more blatant ways. Some of the activities which are supposed to represent 'development', some large and under-utilized infrastructure projects, some excessively luxurious schools and hospitals in urban areas, investment in universities to which access is virtually limited to graduates from fee-paying secondary schools, some industries producing luxury consumer goods, as well as other activities which obviously do not represent development, particularly luxury blocks of flats and large military establishments, use up scarce resources and benefit the privileged few. It is also hard to avoid the impression that some large and conspicuous 'development projects' are undertaken precisely because they do not affect present economic relationships in any drastic way, or are merely intended to distract attention from the government's inability or unwillingness to make more fundamental improvements in the social and economic situation of the people.

There is little real sense of urgency. Naturally there is not a very wide-spread disposition to be concerned with what will happen in, say, twenty years' time. Some of the changes which many people consider to be necessary in the long-run are likely to take effect only slowly, or to cause disruption which should possibly be got over with as soon as possible. The first is true of measures to control the increase in population, administrative reforms, and so on. The second is, arguably, true of land reform. Most land reforms, unless they have been very partial and/or very expensive, have at first caused drops in production. In addition, while there is uncertainty over the extent of the probable reform, the present owners of land are unlikely to invest in it; this is an argument used by the opponents of land reform, but it could equally lead to the conclusion that the reform should be immediate, rather than gradual. In some cases the policy of a very careful and slow land reform, which is officially justified on the grounds that production must not be allowed to fall, may in fact proceed more from a reluctance to confront land-owners, combined with a fundamental underestimate of the capacities of peasants. Arguments for delay on the grounds of the burden on public finances might, again, lead to the conclusion that the reform should be immediate but that the compensation should be postponed, or reduced, or abolished, a conclusion which is as unacceptable to reformist Latin-American governments as it is to the international agencies.[16]

In any case, although Latin-American governments are more immediately threatened by, and sometimes more aware of, the consequences of failure to improve the conditions of life of the poor, and are also concerned with their own survival and therefore must in some cases yield to popular pressures, they share the international agencies' interest in maintaining the *status quo*. Although they complain, on nationalist grounds, of the dominance exercised by foreign companies, of their lack of freedom of manoeuvre, and of the economic losses imposed on them by their dependence, they are also aware of the dangerous consequences to themselves of breaking their relationship with the United States and the international agencies, and losing their support. The fact that they do not repudiate their debts, do not nationalize foreign investments, and in general avoid open defiance of the United States, can be explained partly by fear of United States retaliation, but also by the fear that such actions might lead to uncontrollable internal changes, against which the local élites could no longer invoke foreign intervention.

16. On systems of land tenure and on the progress, or lack of progress, in land reform, see especially the series of country studies published by CIDA (Comité Interamericano de Desarrollo Agrícola).

The security of foreign interests and of the interests of the present governing classes in Latin America are closely interconnected.

Again the economic difficulties of Latin-American countries have been traced to their balance of payments problems, and in particular to the deterioration in their terms of trade. But without fundamental changes in the distribution of income which could reduce demand for imported consumer goods, and possibly the abandonment of some existing industries producing luxury consumption goods and dependent on imported machinery and spare parts, or fundamental changes in the financial and commercial relationships with industrialized countries, the ability of Latin-American governments to solve their balance of payments problems is limited. Foreign exchange is needed in increasing amounts not only for growth but for the functioning of existing industries, for imports of food, and possibly to help in controlling inflation. In Latin-American countries which have problems of financial instability there is often little further scope for the reduction of 'inessential' imports of consumer goods through import substitution, since they are already produced in the country. Generally the industries producing them are highly protected and inefficient, and may have increased rather than decreased foreign exchange requirements, even on the assumption that their output would have been imported if they had not existed; but their continued existence has become a vested interest of local, or foreign, capitalists; and they provide some employment in countries unable to provide it elsewhere.[17] An increasing proportion of Latin-American

17. See for example I.M.D. Little, M. Scott, and T. Scitowsky, *Industry and Trade in Some Developing Countries*, OECD, 1970. See also O. Braun and L. Joy, 'A Model of Economic Stagnation – A Case Study of Argentina', *Economic Journal*, December 1968. Attempts

countries' total foreign exchange receipts is absorbed by the servicing of their foreign debt and by an outflow of capital and profits resulting from reliance on foreign loans, from foreign private investment, and from precautionary investments abroad by Latin-American citizens.

At the same time Latin-American countries have considerable difficulties in increasing their receipts of foreign exchange. Most of their exports are primary commodities whose prices are largely determined by the policies of other countries, including the developed countries; these prices have an extreme tendency to fluctuate, and possibly a long-run tendency to decline in relation to the prices of manufactured goods. For many of these commodities the prospects of increased world consumption are limited; sometimes an increase in the volume of exports results merely in a decline in foreign exchange receipts, either for the country concerned or for developing countries as a whole. In some cases the level of production itself of a country's main exports is controlled by foreign companies, who must be offered expensive inducements to produce more with no guarantee that these will be successful, since their decisions are influenced by a number of other political and international factors. The development of alternative exports is unlikely to be achieved on a significant scale in the short run. In many cases, efforts to diversify primary commodity exports mean simply that one country produces, in less favourable conditions, a commodity which another country is already having difficulty in selling; foreign experts tell

---

to adopt liberalization policies designed in part to bring about the closing down or reform of inefficient import-substituting industries are likely to be ineffective in societies where the government is vulnerable to the activities of powerful pressure groups, local or foreign; cf. for example the case of Brazil, and the special treatment of the motor-car industries.

Colombia to grow cocoa and Ghana to grow coffee. Developing new exports of manufactured goods, even when prices and quality are competitive, takes time. In any case, when a country does succeed in exporting processed or manufactured goods in significant quantities, there is a large probability that it will meet with obstruction in the markets of developed countries; the developed countries have, and use, the power to take unilateral action to protect their agriculture or their industries against what they describe as 'unfair' competition; they may also force developing countries themselves to take action to reduce their exports. Much the same applies to the developed countries' monopoly in shipping and insurance. Moreover Latin-American countries' main industries are likely to be in the hands of subsidiaries of foreign companies, who have usually invested to preserve their access to individual Latin-American markets, and may not be interested in exporting to other countries in which they also have markets or manufacturing interests to protect.

Latin-American governments which want to maintain existing economic relationships are therefore likely to be forced to resort to the international agencies' remedies for balance of payments problems: deflation, devaluation, and efforts to increase the inflow of foreign capital. Devaluation is unlikely to enable them to increase their exports of primary products; it will merely reduce their receipts, unless they impose export taxes; and deflation may hinder plans to produce other goods for export. Increases in foreign private investment and aid can do something to solve short-term problems, but will add to countries' debt burden and, in the case of foreign private investment, may rapidly lead to an outflow of repatriated profits greater than the original inflow. Moreover the amounts of new foreign resources available, either officially or privately, are becoming increasingly inadequate and irrelevant. More specifically, gross inflows of official and private capital to Latin America as a whole are now exceeded by gross outflows of profits, repatriated and expatriated capital, repayments and interest, as the table on pp. 174-5, reproduced from ECLA's *Economic Survey of Latin America, 1966*, shows.[18]

A further complication for governments relying on an inflow of foreign capital to solve their balance of payments problems is the unpredictability of the inflow. Its availability is likely to be affected less by economic policies in Latin America than by quite extraneous political circumstances or by the developed countries' domestic concerns. A country which adjusts its economic policies to satisfy the international agencies and foreign investors is not thereby assured of full support even from the former. Not only may aid be reduced, or altogether stopped, if the country fails to achieve the required degree of financial and monetary equilibrium within the required period; but the United States may react to some minor harassment of its private citizens, the IDA may have to stop disbursements because its funds are not replenished and all three agencies may be affected by political events. The chances of success of policies urged by the international agencies, such as devaluation or import liberalization, may thus be nullified. All this is in addition to the other disadvantages, described above, of adopting the international agencies' policies.

The prospects for growth and stability, combined with the preservation of existing economic relationships and real improvements in general standards of living, seem bleak. The United States has more or less abandoned such official

18. See also Dragoslav Avramovic, 'External Sources of Financing for Latin American Growth', paper prepared for the Conference on The Next Decade of Latin American Development, Cornell University, Ithaca, New York, 20–22 April 1966 (mimeographed).

Latin America: net contribution of external funds to the capacity to import 1960–66

($ million)

Year	Net external autonomous and compensatory funds less amortization payments A	Interest on external loans, profits, and other payments on foreign investment B	Net contribution to the capacity to import C(=A – B)
	LATIN AMERICA (excluding Cuba)		
1960	1,585·2	1,253·6	331·6
1961	1,746·2	1,439·1	307·1
1962	1,509·3	1,483·0	26·3
1963	1,359·7	1,457·1	−97·4
1964	1,807·5	1,704·0	103·5
1965	1,010·6	1,893·6	−883·0
1966		2,049·6	
	BRAZIL		
1960	553·0	198·0	355·0
1961	454·0	187·0	267·0
1962	471·0	202·0	269·0
1963	286·0	147·0	89·0
1964	76·0	191·0	−115·0
1965	−28·0	268·0	−296·0
1966			
	VENEZUELA		
1960	−171·5	533·3	−704·8
1961	−145·0	597·0	−742·0
1962	−357·0	643·0	−1,000·0
1963	−159·0	627·0	−786·0
1964	4·0	700·0	−696·0
1965	144·0	747·0	−603·0
1966			

Year	Net external autonomous and compensatory funds less amortization payments A	Interest on external loans, profits, and other payments on foreign investment B	Net contribution to the capacity to import C(=A – B)
	MEXICO		
1960	194·4	190·5	3·9
1961	406·0	204·0	202·0
1962	228·0	237·0	−9·0
1963	359·0	266·0	93·0
1964	711·0	324·0	387·0
1965	201·0	339·0	−138·0
1966			
	ARGENTINA		
1960	696·1	88·4	607·7
1961	327·2	165·8	161·4
1962	234·6	80·1	154·5
1963	43·5	71·5	−28·0
1964	−131·4	113·2	−244·6
1965	−132·2	94·8	−227·0
1966			
	LATIN AMERICA (excluding Argentina, Brazil, Cuba, Mexico and Venezuela)		
1960	313·2	243·4	69·8
1961	704·0	285·3	418·7
1962	932·7	320·9	611·8
1963	880·2	345·6	534·6
1964	1147·9	375·8	772·1
1965	825·8	444·8	381·0
1966		575·6	

Source: ECLA, Economic Survey of Latin America, 1966, and IMF, Balance of Payments Yearbook, Vols. 17 and 18.

interest as there was in Alliance for Progress reforms. United States officials sometimes justify this abandonment by pointing to the unwillingness of Latin-American ruling classes to concern themselves with development and reform. But at the same time their policies are aimed at the protection of these ruling classes against social change. The United States government claims to be fighting a 'war on two fronts': one against subversion, the other against poverty. But the former is increasingly emphasized; and a concerted effort is being made to build up the counter-insurgency capacity of the armed forces in Latin America and the Caribbean. Military take-overs, ostensibly to restore political and financial order, have taken place in Bolivia, Brazil, Argentina and, with some interesting variations, in Peru. Within Latin America many people therefore see revolution as the real alternative to stagnation and repression.

(ii) *Revolution*

Supposing it is true that neither policies of the sort favoured by the international agencies, nor reformist policies of the sort discussed in the last section, are likely to provide substantial improvements in the general well-being of most Latin Americans, some consideration needs to be given to what the alternatives, to be achieved through revolution, might be. Rather than attempting to put forward any particular proposals for revolutionary change, or to define what is meant by revolution, this study attempts to give some indication of what can perhaps be expected from a revolution in Latin America by examining briefly the case of Cuba.[19]

19. There are two other countries in Latin America, Bolivia and Mexico, which have had what might be described as 'genuine' revolutions. But in Bolivia the effects of the 1952 revolution have been largely

In Cuba there exists an example of what can be achieved in ten years of revolution, in spite of an economic blockade by the United States and in spite of the exceptional previous dependence of the Cuban economy on the United States. The Cuban revolution has not so far been particularly successful, as far as can be ascertained from published statistics, in increasing the average levels of production of material goods; there have been big increases in the production of some goods, declines in the production of others, and in a few years probably an overall decline in national product, as usually defined. In addition Cuba has received large amounts of aid from the Soviet Union and socialist countries; but the figures usually quoted include the effects of the higher prices paid by the Soviet Union for Cuba's exports of sugar, prices which exceed residual 'world' market prices in roughly the same orders of magnitude as those previously paid by the United States; they include also aid for imports of spare parts and sometimes replacements for Cuba's almost exclusively United States equipment and machinery, some of which was made unusable by the trade embargo; and to some extent the aid merely replaces previously available sources of foreign capital. Finally it is true that the revolution is, in some ways,

___

nullified, partly as a result of direct United States pressures; see Laurence Whitehead, *The United States and Bolivia, A Case of Neo-Colonialism*, The Haslemere Group, 515 Liverpool Road, London, N1, 1969. In Mexico the recent long period of stability and growth has often been ascribed to the 1920 revolution and its subsequent effects (see also this chapter, note 3); but inequalities of income and political repression are now increasing and are accompanied by increased foreign private investment and a dependence on tourist revenue and good relations with the United States. 'Revolution' is an abused word; it has also, for example, been used by Presidents Frei, Castelo Branco and Onganía to describe the quite unrevolutionary activities of their governments.

and especially in comparison with the luxuries and corruption of pre-revolutionary Havana, austere. It is estimated that Cuba is currently investing 30 per cent or more of its national income; efforts are being made to export a larger proportion of Cuban production; imports, especially of consumer goods, are severely restricted; and most Cubans, especially government officials, work extraordinarily hard. The revolution has above all meant more effort; it has created a will to develop the country's resources and to ensure that the whole population works for, is involved in, and benefits from this development that is not apparent elsewhere in Latin America.

It is hard to evaluate the results of these efforts in terms of economic development.[20] But some remarkable features of the Cuban revolution can be indicated. The revolution has, for example, virtually eliminated unemployment, which is estimated to have involved 50 per cent of the agricultural population except during the three months of the sugar harvest, and whose average annual rate in 1956–7, a 'good' year, is calculated to have been 16 per cent.[21] It has achieved a very great degree of equality in the distribution of income. It provides all Cubans with a minimum wage which is more

20. There is a lack of published material on economic development in Cuba, particularly of a sort that lays any claim to objectivity. But see Dudley Seers, editor, *Cuba, the Economic and Social Revolution*, The University of North Carolina Press, 1964, which is to be brought up to date; René Dumont, *Cuba, Socialisme et Développement*, série Frontière Ouverte, Paris, 1964; Michel Gutelman, *L'Agriculture socialisée à Cuba*, Paris, François Maspero, 1967.

21. See Dudley Seers (op. cit. previous note), p. 12. This achievement is largely the result of more regular employment in agriculture and new employment in industry and construction. It can be ascribed only to a small extent to increases in the armed forces, and probably not at all to increases in bureaucratic employment; the Cubans have burnt desks rather than adding to them.

than enough to buy everything that is available on the ration, and therefore to provide adequate food and clothing for many who were previously without them, and to have money left over for travel and restaurants. It has more or less eliminated illiteracy, provided primary and secondary education for nearly the whole of the school-age population, introduced imaginative and modern methods in schools and universities, eliminated or greatly reduced many diseases, and extended medical and educational services into remote and previously neglected rural areas. Finally, quite extraordinary efforts, physical and intellectual, are being devoted to modernization and the applying of new techniques in agriculture, and in rural areas in general.

The success in providing jobs for nearly all Cubans is impressive in view of the current pessimism about the possibility of increasing employment in other developing countries, and the fact that levels of unemployment, overt and 'disguised', appear to be increasing elsewhere in Latin America. Another achievement rather exclusive to Cuba is that the benefits of development, and the activities of skilled people, are now much more widely spread throughout the country, thus greatly reducing the disproportionate preponderance of Havana in population and wealth, and the accompanying misery and shanty-towns. Similarly, the very large increases in expenditure of a 'social' or 'non-productive' nature, on education and health in particular, but also in fields such as housing and pensions, are in marked contrast with the achievements and objectives elsewhere, and in particular with the policy recommendations of the international agencies. These expenditures have been accompanied by investment of the 'productive' nature sometimes favoured by the international agencies, particularly in agriculture, which, although the figures are again extremely inadequate is almost certainly higher in proportion to national income than in other Latin-American countries. This has been possible mainly because of restrictions on luxury consumption and on the expatriation of capital by Cubans and foreigners,[22] and because of the expropriation of profitable industries and services, resulting from the revolution.

Finally, although the importance of increases in levels of production is much emphasized in Cuba, such increases are not the only objectives of policy. It is often assumed as self-evident, by the international agencies in particular,[23] that the major purpose of 'development' is to increase output. The distribution and nature of this output, and the nature of society as a whole, are neglected. There is also a tendency to assume that 'economic' questions can be considered in isolation.[24] The most significant achievements of the Cuban revolution are probably in the social field, in the much greater equality and in the abolition or erosion of hierarchical and oppressive relationships, in the degree to which Cubans participate in and approve of the decisions of society, in the great increases in political and cultural awareness and activity among Cubans. In some cases such objectives conflict with the achievement of rapid increases

22. On the outflow of capital from Cuba before the revolution see, for example, the World Bank report on Cuba, published by the Johns Hopkins Press, 1950, p. 518.

23. See, for example, chapter 2, note 4, quoting Irving S. Friedman of the World Bank, especially the sentence 'And accelerating development, of course, comes down to questions of increasing productive capacity and increasing economic efficiency within the countries that are members of the World Bank.'

24. An example is the widespread attitude among Western economists to the rebellion in Pakistan and the overthrow of President Ayub Khan, which were regarded as an irritating setback, of an external nature, to economic policies which were showing signs of 'success'.

in the output of material goods and of greater economic 'efficiency', as it is usually defined in market economies. Thus Guevara said: 'Underdevelopment and the customary flight of capital to "civilized" countries make rapid change without sacrifices impossible. There still remains a long stretch to be covered in the building of the economic base, and the temptation to follow the beaten paths of material interest as the lever of speedy development is very great.'[25] 'It is not a question of how many kilograms of meat are eaten or how many times a year someone may go on holiday to the seashore or how many pretty imported things can be bought with present wages. It is rather that the individual feels greater fulfilment, that he has greater inner wealth and many more responsibilities.'[26]

But Cuba receives support from none of the Washington-based international agencies; the United States still attempts to sabotage Cuban efforts.[27] Why? Basically because Cuba has nationalized United States interests, and the United

25. From his essay 'Man and Socialism in Cuba', written in 1965 and reproduced in *Venceremos, The Speeches and Writings of Ernesto Che Guevara*, edited by John Gerassi, Weidenfeld and Nicolson, 1968, p. 391.   26. ibid., p. 398

27. The following is an extract from US Congressional Hearings:
'*Congressman Thomson*. Do you think it is impossible to get a few guerillas in there that might lob a mortar shell onto some strategic point one day, and the next day lob one on some other point, and create a little confusion in Cuba? I don't mean a major confrontation.
General Draper. (Security deletion.)
Congressman Thomson. Well I would think if the Vietnamese can mortar Danang then somebody could mortar some place in Cuba if we really wanted to do it. Now may be it is not worthwhile.
General Draper. (Security deletion.)
Congressman Thomson. Yes, let's hope that is continued.'
(House Foreign Affairs Committee, Hearings on Hemispheric Relations, 15263, pp. 839–40, 4 April 1968.)

States is not prepared to take the risk of this happening elsewhere in Latin America. But nationalization of United States and other foreign interests is an inevitable accompaniment of a social transformation of the sort that has been carried out in Cuba. It is inconceivable that any Latin-American country will free itself of the dominance and misappropriation of resources exercised by groups of its own citizens but fail to free itself from that of foreigners. The size of most developing countries' foreign debt, and of remittances of profits and interest abroad, and the fact that it can be demonstrated that they would benefit substantially, in economic terms, from expropriating foreign investments and repudiating their debts,[28] make it still clearer that governments will not take action against their own country's élite without also taking action against foreigners. Some of the United States' disillusion with the Alliance for Progress stems from this impossibility.[29] The United States is not prepared to follow the ideas embodied in the Alliance for Progress to their logical conclusion, by admitting the possibility of nationalization of foreign investments; not surprisingly, since the Alliance for Progress was intended to remove the danger of this happening. Moreover, since the Cuban revolution, the United States has been more wary than ever of governments which might follow the Cuban path. There is a general bias against all

28. See for example forthcoming book by R. B. Sutcliffe on Industry and Underdevelopment.

29. Programmes to redistribute land and property in Latin America are acceptable, on the whole, and indeed encouraged, so long as they do not affect United States interests. There are many examples. One which occurred recently (in 1968) was in Colombia, where the agricultural reform agency, after having expropriated with compensation a number of Colombian land-owners, attempted to expropriate on the same terms some property of a US timber company. The US embassy threatened to cut aid.

policies and events in developing countries which appear to contain the danger of a move towards socialism.[30]

ALTERNATIVE POLICIES IN AID

Obviously the threat of cutting aid, except as an indication of worse things to come, is not likely to have much effect, one way or the other, on the prospects of revolution in Latin America. It is true that the loss of aid, and of access to traditional sources of credit and supply, can cause difficult problems of transition. Although dependence on imports, especially luxury imports or imports for the maintenance of factories producing luxury goods, will be reduced, some imports remain essential. For example there will be a continuing need to import spare parts for existing industries which need to be maintained, raw materials such as oil, which are not available locally, machinery for new investment, and technical expertise of various kinds. The capacity of other socialist countries to supply these needs is limited. The difficulties of increasing export earnings are, as has been said, considerable. On the other hand many Latin American countries would on balance benefit, even from a short term financial point of view, from nationalizing foreign industries, repudiating their debts, and preventing the outflow of capital, interest and profits, so long as this merely resulted in their losing access to new foreign loans and investment. And in the long term it is clearly necessary that underdeveloped countries should reduce their dependence on the industrialized countries and the concomitant opportunities

30. As United States policies in the Dominican Republic and Guyana, for example, have shown. On Guyana, see forthcoming article by Colin Henfrey in *Patterns of Foreign Influence in the Caribbean*, edited by Emmanuel de Kadt, Oxford University Press.

for the latter to exploit them. In this sense it could be said that the loss of 'aid' was an advantage. In addition, of course, the cutting of aid is merely a minimum response to a revolutionary situation; the other sanctions of imperialism, commercial and military, are those which really need to be faced and dealt with. The question of aid is therefore relatively unimportant.

But some of those who agree with some or all of the criticisms of the major aid agencies in this study may nevertheless think that it would be realistic to argue for reforms in aid, and to demand that aid should be available to countries even if, in the course of a revolution for example, they should happen to displease the ruling classes of the industrialized countries. It is therefore necessary to discuss the possibility of such reforms.

It might, for example, be suggested that the existing international agencies should change their policies, or that new international institutions should be set up; that the allocation of resources should be determined primarily or wholly by the less developed countries; that the influence of the agencies responsible for allocating the resources should be confined to the selection and supervision of projects financed by them; that international agencies should become involved in a 'dialogue' about countries' general policies and the use of resources, but should not make the size or continuation of their financial contribution conditional on any particular policies being adopted; or that resources should be allocated automatically, according to a formula based primarily on the size of population.

Most of these suggestions are, however, unrealistic. Some hope might be pinned to the idea that resources should be transferred according to an automatic formula, which would be determined in advance, and by an agency with no discretionary powers, roughly on the principle of taxation. The principles of unconditional allocations of resources has already been partially accepted in the agreement on IMF Special Drawing Rights; at first it was proposed that Special Drawing Rights should be allocated only to developed countries, on the grounds that developing countries would not use them 'responsibly', but it was eventually agreed that they should be allocated to all members of the IMF in proportion to their quotas. This principle could in theory be extended. Moreover it was originally intended that the Fund's own resources should be more or less automatically available to members;[31] a return to this intention is perhaps conceivable. It is marginally more likely that developed countries would tolerate the idea of resources being transferred to countries of whose policies they disapproved if the resources were transferred automatically than if they were transferred bilaterally, or through an institution with discretionary powers which they could influence. But this idea suffers, like the other suggestions, from the gross improbability that developed countries will relinquish their power to use the threat to withhold 'aid' in order to promote their own economic and political interests, or that they would consider it worth their while to transfer resources once they were deprived of this power.

Objections to the other alternatives are possibly more basic. To begin with the possibility that the international agencies will change their policies, or be replaced by other institutions with a different set of policies and priorities: enough has presumably been said, especially in chapter 2, to show that there are limits to how far the existing institutions can change. The same limitations would be likely to apply to any alternative international institution. It is true that the experience with CIAP, with the regional development banks, especially the Inter-American Development Bank, and even

31. See chapter 2, section on the IMF.

with the World Bank itself, in so far as it is international, has shown that there is some desire on the part of developed countries to internationalize the transfer of resources and also to persuade others, including the developing countries themselves, to play some part in scrutinizing policies and allocating the resources accordingly. This is especially so in the United States, where the emphasis on 'good performance' is strongest and where the CIAP's functions are compared to those of the Organization for European Economic Co-operation in playing a part in decisions about Marshall Aid. But the United States' basic reason for promoting international institutions is to transfer some of the responsibility for making unpleasant decisions on to others; it has no desire for the decisions themselves to be different. Moreover the CIAP, in spite of Latin-American pressure, has not been permitted to control the allocation of the resources provided by the United States under the Alliance for Progress; the most it can hope to do is to *persuade* the United States, and others, to allocate their resources in accordance with its views, whatever they may be. The IADB probably demonstrates the limits of freedom of action likely to be achieved by an agency actually responsible for allocating a considerable proportion of 'aid'. It has nevertheless on the whole avoided controversial issues; Cuba is no longer a member, and receives no aid from the Bank; and where the IADB has attempted to influence general policies, it has done so in support of, or on lines similar to, the other agencies. The efforts of the developing countries to set up a United Nations financial agency in which their votes would be predominant have been unsuccessful. The resources of the United Nations specialized or technical agencies are small; and although the Soviet Union and Cuba are members, the influence of the United States on the ideology and policies of United

Nations specialized agencies, such as the FAO, remains considerable. The difficulties in obtaining finance for the African Development Bank, with its professed desire for independence and refusal of directors from outside Africa, are significant, especially in comparison with the experience of the more co-operative Asian Development Bank.[32] It is very unlikely that any international institution with large financial resources, necessarily supplied by the major industrial powers, could achieve any real independence and autonomy in its decisions.

An alternative which might be suggested is that the amounts of resources to be allocated to particular countries should be based on a formula determined in advance, but that their use should be determined, not by the national governments receiving them, but internationally. This idea has certain attractions for those who are concerned about 'wasting' aid. No attempt would be made to influence the country's general policies, but governments would, in theory, be prevented from misusing the resources provided. However, experience has shown that external supervision of the use of 'aid', even by the most respected international agencies, has not invariably prevented any but the most extreme forms of waste; projects which seem carefully prepared and supervised may nevertheless have a negative social or economic return; and external supervision of the choice of projects leads as often as not to distortions of priorities in the allocation of resources, especially when there is a refusal to make resources available for any but the direct import costs of the project, and when there is excessive emphasis on its financial viability as opposed to its contribution to development in general. The idea is more-

32. See John White, 'The Asian Development Bank: A Question of Style', *International Affairs*, Vol. 44, No. 4, October 1968; and also his forthcoming ODI publication on regional development banks.

over not very practical, for if the country is assured of receiving the financial resources in any case, it is difficult to force it to use them for any particular purposes. The apparently simpler idea, that allocation should be based not on an automatic formula but on the availability of 'good projects', is already claimed by some governments and agencies to determine their allocation policies, partly or wholly, and was in the past broadly the policy of the World Bank.[33] But, as soon as there is an excess of 'good' projects over available resources, this idea suffers from much the same disadvantages as the attempt to allocate resources according to some view of the country's general policies. How is it possible to judge whether a certain sum would be better spent on a hospital in Turkey or a school in Ghana, without taking into account a number of other general and political factors?

It has also been suggested that the agencies concerned with the transfer of resources should become involved in a 'dialogue' with developing countries.[34] According to this view, such agencies should as far as possible be involved in planning decisions, and they should provide the critical appraisal of these decisions which is sometimes lacking in developing countries. But they should not press for the adoption of any particular policies, and they should indeed be prepared to change their advice if they found it too readily accepted. Presumably they would favour countries which were prepared to discuss their policies with them; but they should not make their financial contribution dependent on the acceptance of their opinions, as is now the

33. Within the limits imposed by its nature as a Bank, promoting the flow of international investment.

34. See John White, *Pledged to Development*, ODI, 1967, and Andrzej Krassowski, *The Aid Relationship*, ODI, 1968. (See also chapter 1, note 11.)

case. Again, it seems rather unrealistic to expect the present situation to change. If there is no conditionality involved, and if the bargaining position of the aid agencies is not to be reinforced by the fact that they have control over the allocation of resources, it is hard to see what special advantages there are in governments discussing their policies with them, as opposed to anybody else. In any case, no international agency respected and financially supported by the developed countries could give even advice which the latter considered incompatible with their essential interests. There are limits to what even the CIAP, with no control over the allocation of resources, is permitted to say. The CIAP can perform a mediating role between expansionist or reformist Latin-American governments and the international agencies; it can perhaps improve the situation in some respects. But its role is limited. It has in fact little, if any, more authority than the many other advisers of developing countries. This is because it does not have the financial power to impose its views either on the international agencies or on Latin-American governments. If it did, its views, such as they are, would have to change. An attempt to link the giving of advice with the provision of aid is likely, in the nature of things, to result in an attempt to impose the point of view of the provider.

It is of course conceivable that the developed countries, and therefore the agencies allocating aid, will change their attitude. For example, it is possible to imagine them, as the AID did in the early 1960s, putting more emphasis on social policies, on the redistribution of income, and so on, and in general being more 'progressive' than they now are. But, as argued in the section 'Reforms' in this chapter, it is unlikely that such policies can be effective without radical changes affecting the position of powerful local and foreign interests. And, in the absence of a fundamental change of attitude in the United States and other developed countries towards their investments and other interests in the Third World, perhaps only conceivable as a result of internal changes in the former, such changes will still be excluded from the range of acceptable policies. Whether they could become acceptable depends partly on the extent to which the survival and development of capitalist societies is dependent on their ability to invest in, and trade with, developing countries, and to do so in present conditions. Many of the arguments of the supporters of 'aid' and 'leverage' rest on the assumption that the interests of the governments and peoples of industrialized and non-industrialized countries are compatible; but, at any rate in present conditions, they frequently conflict. Moreover if socialist developing countries were to receive aid, this would require not only that their policies be acceptable, but that there should exist some motive other than the pre-servation of investments, trading interests and general 'order' and 'stability' which would be powerful enough to induce industrialized countries to transfer resources; it is not clear what this motive could be.

Finally, even supposing it is argued that the policies favoured by industrialized countries are or might be-come conducive to development and progress in non-industrialized countries, there remain potential disadvantages in any attempts by the former to influence the latter. First, whatever the nature and views of the governments or agencies providing resources, there is likely to be a con-tinuing temptation for them to use the opportunity provided by 'aid' to promote their own political and commercial interests, so long as they retain discretion or influence over its use, even if this is at the expense of other policies con-sidered desirable. Second, and more fundamentally, the whole principle of the staff of an external agency attempting to use the agency's financial power to determine the policies to be followed in large areas of the world is dubious. At the moment, such an attempt is being made by organizations which are quite unrepresentative of opinion in these areas. But, even if the organizations became more representative, there would still be formidable objections to an organization using its financial power in such a way. How would its staff be selected? What would their qualifications and inclinations be? How well would they need to know the varying conditions and traditions of different countries and regions? How, in any case, could they take these into account? Above all, how would 'good performance' be defined? For the sake of fairness, would it be necessary to evolve one or two relatively easily measurable but necessarily crude criteria of good performance[35] which could be applied to all countries? If not, how would it be possible to avoid wholly subjective judgements by individual members of the staff of the organization? How could they compare their judgements with each others'? Even within Latin America, for instance, one of the most usual mistakes made is an attempt to generalize about the continent's problems and solutions. Generalized solutions, when they are propounded, must necessarily fail to take account of some of the most important realities and priorities, and may neglect large and important areas of the economy and society. Unless it were possible to produce a much more neutral and clear definition of 'good performance' than now exists, and unless allocation was based primarily on population and income levels, the probability is that the allocation of aid would continue to be determined mainly by the political preferences and special interests of its allocators. For the moment, therefore,

35. Such as the World Bank's 'percentage of public investment financed from savings on current account'? Which of course presupposes a particular form of economic organization.

the realistic alternatives are the present, politically determined, policies of the international agencies, or no aid.

These negative conclusions are based on observation of the functioning of the existing economic and social system. Under socialism, and with the principles of international solidarity operating in full vigour, things will be different. But that would be the subject of a different book, and might sound utopian to those made cynical by capitalism.

APPENDIX: THE BIRTH AND DEATH OF
AN ODI STUDY

THE World Bank, for reasons best known to itself, decided to finance a series of Overseas Development Institute studies. The ODI assumed that it was supposed to evaluate and publicize the Bank's activities, and it suggested that I should produce the second study in the series.[1] The study was to concentrate on the Bank's activities in Latin America, an area newly in vogue in British academic and business circles.

Before I went to Latin America, a project was submitted to, and accepted by, the World Bank, stating among other things that the study proposed to concentrate on 'activities which involve a fairly close relationship between the international agencies and Latin-American countries' and on 'an examination of the potential role of international institutions and of economic aid as catalysts in development, assuming that more is involved than a simple transfer of resources or the setting up of isolated projects'.

However, after I had done most of my research, the Bank staff discovered, belatedly, that they had an objection to anything being written on the subject of 'leverage' irrespective of its conclusions. I thus had some personal experience of Bank methods: I was summoned to an interview at which an attempt was made to force me to abandon my research and to write about 'something else'. The Bank felt that it could operate less effectively if it was publicly known to be engaged in the business of leverage; an analogy was

1. The first in the series was *Pledged to Development*, by John White, ODI. 1967.

drawn with 'secret diplomacy'. I came out of this interview battered, but eventually realized that I was in a position not to be bullied out of my research; I had a lot of material on the Bank's activities, and merely wanted to hear from them their version.

So the Information Department agreed to arrange a series of appointments for me. I saw all the Bank officials whom I had asked to see. With one exception: the official most concerned with Colombia fled. Some of these interviews were helpful and informative; several lasted well over an hour, or were repeated on subsequent occasions. But the usual attitude was one of more or less hostile, more or less veiled, suspicion. My interview with the Head of the Western Hemisphere Department was devoted almost exclusively to unsolicited explanations of why the Bank preferred the public not to know about leverage, and also to an attempt to discover what my conclusions would be if, in spite of everything, I persisted in my desire to write about leverage.

I had even less success with the IMF, with whom the ODI had no institutional links. I obtained an interview with only one of the senior IMF officials whom I asked to see through official channels, although I met a number of IMF officials unofficially. The AID, on the other hand, was helpful; its officials, who are frequently academics on short assignments, talked to me at length and with relative frankness, and I saw most of the senior officials whom I had wanted to see. Similarly, Latin-American politicians and officials were on the whole very accessible and very willing to talk about their negotiations with the international agencies.

I produced the first draft of the study, apart from a short concluding chapter, in June 1968. The response of the new Director of ODI was brief; 'for all he knew' I might be right in my criticisms, but 'frankly' he thought the study

would be dismissed 'by serious readers and reviewers
alike'. A memorandum from the Director of Studies, sent
to me in July, was more tactfully expressed; he thought I
had 'produced a document that is written with considerable
power', and said: 'You obviously feel very deeply about
the matters you are discussing and I think the critique you
are building up is a most original and important approach
to these matters. But ... I feel bound to make a number of
criticisms. ... This is not because I object to your taking the
particular line you have ...'

The Director of Studies wanted me to provide some more
factual information, of an elementary variety. In addition,
he 'got the impression' that I 'regarded [the international
agencies] as one great "plot"'. Further, '... My impression
from your draft is that you feel that monetary stability, the
acceptance of past contractual obligations (and particularly
those concerned with debts), social and economic change
brought about rather slowly in a gentlemanly sort of way,
etc., are all characteristics that need to be thrown over ...'
He had a 'suspicion' that I might think it would be to
Chile's economic advantage to do without aid and foreign
investment, to nationalize US assets and to default on
debts. I did not define what I meant by 'radical solutions'.
'Is it revolution ...? If it is I think you need to argue far
more effectively that the slower evolution, with respect for
more "traditional" values, is not only wrong but less
desirable than what you are proposing ...' He also thought
my style had 'the touch of enlightened Sunday paper
journalism. The best ones of course, but none-the-less still
the Sundays. ... From time to time I kept on thinking I
was reading Nora Beloff red hot from Paris about some
vital conference that had just taken place ...' He detected
some 'rather loaded innuendo. For example ... "This hope
is encouraged by the international agencies, who *of course*

(my italics) believe in the role of foreign capital in promoting development."' I had written 'a rather polemical document' to 'show up' that private investment, the USA and the international agencies were 'baddies'.

Further ODI proposals were that my conclusions, which in the first draft were at the beginning, should instead go at the end. It was some months before the ODI agreed to circulate the draft for comments.

The World Bank's comments on the first draft, which arrived in November, were voluminous. They were spattered with allegations of 'inaccuracy', but, with one or two exceptions, the criticisms were not concerned with facts, but with interpretation, 'distortion' or 'bias', and with the effect the study would be likely to make on the Bank's image. Mr Irving Friedman, from the office of the President, in a note addressed to the Bank's Information Department, said: '... I would hope that ODI would give very careful thought to publishing such a document. My main concern is whether it gives the impression that what the agencies do is wrong ...'

A similarly senior official, in the Bank's Western Hemisphere Department, who was personally sympathetic and helpful to me, hoped, in a note to the Information Department, that the study 'could be quietly buried'. In a six-page letter to me, he said he knew me 'well enough to know that your own opinions are sincerely held'. But he thought my evidence was inadequate. The following is a sample of his criticisms:

Let me take you to task here over some of the assertions you make, and try to show you why I think you are constantly distorting the evidence to fit your thesis.

On page 6 of chapter 1 you say that one of the basic beliefs of the international agencies seems to be that 'Latin American problems are of a kind which are soluble by fiscal and monetary policies of the IMF variety'. Then, on page 10 of the same chapter, you suggest, as though it were a novel thought, that the major problems of Latin America are not economic but political, that radical social and political changes are needed, and that the international agencies 'are committed to defending the *status quo*'. How do you square these statements with, for example, the following passage from the 1966 Bank Economic Report on Chile?

'The fact that it [i.e. the Report] says little about the social and political aspects of economic development should not be taken to mean that these are considered unimportant. Society in Chile is still structured in such a way that the country's human resources cannot be used effectively, and we believe that the Chilean Government is entirely right in regarding far-reaching social reforms as an indispensable long-run condition of satisfactory economic performance. Agrarian reform is absolutely necessary to revitalize agriculture. The extension of primary and secondary education and the eradication of illiteracy can contribute a lot to higher productivity. Better housing conditions may help to safeguard political stability. These are all appropriate goals for an economic development program, but in allocating resources between different uses Chile has persistently tended to favour social investment (and infrastructural investment in public works) at the expense of more productive investment in industry and agriculture.'[2]

There was much more on my failure to appreciate the Bank's virtues and point of view, and a few points of factual and interpretative error. Finally he concluded:

If there was any chance that the paper was going to be published in anything like its present form, I think that we would

2. The last sentence is crucial. The Bank is prepared to pay lip-service to 'social reforms'. Its actual demands are that such reforms as exist should be curtailed. Note also the reasons for their necessity: 'human resources' must be 'used effectively'; social reforms are a condition of 'satisfactory economic performance'; education can contribute to 'higher productivity'; better housing to 'political stability'.

have to lodge official objections with ODI because publication could be quite awkward to us in our relations with Latin American countries. Certainly, the image you present of the Bank in its dealings with Latin America is a very different image from that which our new President is trying to create.

Another senior Bank commentator stated: 'My advice would be that a major revision of Miss Hayter's book is necessary: whether this can be done, depends on the extent of the revisions that are needed. On this, I am sure the Western Hemisphere Department will have its views.' In his five-page memorandum, he identified 'a sort of code of conduct' demanded by the Bank, to which he thought it was 'difficult to take exception', and which included the following: 'measures conducive to a larger flow of private capital and public funds'; 'not ... too much inflation'; 'full-cost pricing of projects to which [the Bank] lends'; 'not ... large and rapidly growing administrative expenditures'; 'not ... administrative controls over production and prices'; 'a financial plan for [public investment programmes] which does not call for too much suppliers credit financing or too much printing of money'; and 'service payments on ... external debt'.

My official IMF contact, in a letter to me, appreciated my 'courtesy' in sending him a draft. But he could not make 'specific and detailed comments', mainly because

there is so much in the paper that I disagree with that it would not be feasible to attempt to overcome these disagreements by drafting suggestions, and certainly not by point-by-point comments in writing. Moreover, it does not really appear practicable to separate the factual material from the judgements since the former is so co-mingled with opinion, if only by the choice of words, that in almost every line one can guess in what direction the ultimate judgements will go.... I am satisfied that all of us are at one in a deep devotion to the economic development of the developing countries and share the conviction that this is a matter of the highest priority. On our part, however, we recognize that this process is bound to be an arduous one. . . . I am afraid, if your paper were to be distributed or published in its present form, it would not be helpful either to the agencies concerned, including your own, nor to the developing countries.

Finally he offered to comment on a revised draft, and suggested: 'Even better, if you should have occasion to come to Washington again, we could arrange for an oral discussion between you and interested members of our staff.' And he assured me that he appreciated 'the careful effort and thinking and the sincerity with which you have clearly approached this assignment'. I noted with interest the change in the official IMF attitude towards arranging interviews for me with members of the IMF staff.

There followed a discussion with the ODI as to whether I was to produce a new draft of the study. I was willing to meet the stated objections, in particular as far as presentation, factual errors and omissions, and vagueness over what I meant by 'radical changes' were concerned. But I asked repeatedly whether the stated objections were the real objections, and whether political issues were not involved. I was assured that the objections were technical, and that there was no question of there being any objection to my conclusions, or to *what* I said, as opposed to *how* I said it. I was further assured that the decision on publication was a matter for the Director of ODI, with advice from some members of the staff and possibly one or two selected Council members, and was not dependent either on agreement by the ODI's Council, with its preponderance of businessmen representing companies with interests in the Third World, or on agreement by the World Bank.

On this basis I agreed to produce a new draft. I postponed

starting on economics and a new job at Oxford, and I worked on the draft for some time after ODI stopped paying my salary at the end of 1968. It was boring and frustrating work: I was mainly expected to shuffle the study around so as to 'state the agencies' case fairly' at the beginning, and put my own views at the end. The second draft[3] was, in my opinion, not very different from the first. It was a bit longer, and it contained more facts and bibliographical references, especially in chapter two; it was more explicit on certain issues; and it included a section on Cuba, where I had spent five weeks. Also, the first draft, as first drafts tend to, had needed some tidying up; the second draft was a bit tidier. ODI seemed pleased. On 29 April 1969, I received a letter from the Director of Studies, as follows:

Tony and I have been through your draft and I am very pleased to say that we both think it now well on the way to publication by ODI.

There are a number of steps that we now have to take in piloting it through the last stages ...

(1) We shall need to send a copy to someone in the World Bank for comments ...

(2) I am intending to send a copy of the draft to two or three people who have not been substantially involved in the earlier round of comments ...

... (5) Will you have a word with MH/JO to work out a time-table for a possible date for publication? I would not anticipate that the comments from other people would take very long and that their observations will involve you in a great deal of additional work ...

Another ODI comment was that the study was now '*very* much more convincing', but that the section on Cuba was too 'glowing', and should preferably be replaced by 'a list

3. Which, with the amendments mentioned below, is substantially what is published here.

of precise recommendations to the agencies'. I rewrote the section on Cuba, much as it is now, made some more small changes in the light of ODI and other comments, and delivered the draft for, as I hoped, publication.

In July I received a letter from the ODI stating the following: 'Alas we are not home and dry yet, as the IBRD/IMF have written to us recently and raised the whole issue of the use of confidential information .... we have therefore written to them ... and have asked them to be specific where they have any doubts ...' I was subsequently given copies of the IBRD/IMF communications concerned. There was, first, a letter from the Information Department of the Bank, addressed to the Director of the ODI and dated 17 June 1969, as follows:

... First thing on my return I have had the Hayter story in full storm on my desk. I am sending you *unofficially* copies of two memos.

It would be very unpleasant to exert any sort of a veto on publication, but I can see the extreme awkwardness of publishing what Bank people consider very confidential material. Lars Lind did go out of his way to ensure that Teresa saw all the top brass, and that they treated her as a colleague. They not unnaturally expect that their confidences would be respected. Equally I can see that Teresa needs this evidence to make her case, and would suppose that what she had gathered was available evidence. This is a problem that journalists often face and have learnt methods of evasion, which are not known to Teresa as they were to John.

I should add that the opinions of the people who have read the revised draft remain very adverse on the grounds that it remains unbalanced and hence unscholarly. I do not believe that all of these people are of the opinion that we have done no wrong, but they feel we have done some right too.

Then there were the 'two memos'. One was from Mr Alter, head of the Western Hemisphere Department of the

Bank, to the Information Department of the Bank, and was as follows:

1. The IMF called us late last week to express their concern over what they understood to be the ODI's intention to proceed quickly with publication of Miss Hayter's paper....I must say that, like the IMF, I had been assuming that, as a result of the comments we gave you on an earlier draft, steps were being taken to ensure that the paper would not be published in anything like its present form. There have admittedly been quite extensive changes to the draft since we last saw it, including the insertion of a short section on Cuba, but these do not remove the grounds for the objections we raised then ...

2. ... we have not had time to go over it in detail, nor do I think it would be profitable for us to do so, since our objections cannot be met by minor changes in drafting. The real trouble is that the author has tried to bend the facts to suit her thesis, and in the process she has not only got a lot of things wrong, but she has also made quite indiscreet use of information given her in confidence by people with whom she talked in the Bank and the Fund (note, for example, various statements about what is said in Bank economic reports and the reference on page 5 of Chapter 2 to the Bank's Operational Memorandum No. 2.04).

3. Let me draw your attention to a few examples amongst many of passages in the paper which, whether true or false (and most are false), could seriously embarrass the Bank in its relations with its member countries in the Western Hemisphere and could also embarrass the President in his dealings with Executive Directors:

Chapter 2, page 2[4] – 'discussions have also taken place between the missions of the three institutions [IMF, IBRD, AID] in the United States embassy in the country concerned.'

4. The first two passages from chapter 2 quoted in the letter are to be found on pp. 27 and 57 of this book. The third and fourth passages quoted from chapter 2 have been modified or omitted since the memo was written. The quotations from chapter 3 are on pp. 112 and 132 of this book, and those from chapter 4 on pp. 155–6 and 160, note 8. The last passage quoted has since been slightly modified.

Chapter 2, page 27 – 'the Bank's Staff [does] "not inform its Board of Governors or anybody else" of the efforts it is making to improve, in its eyes, the general economic performance of its members.'

Chapter 2, page 41 – 'the Bank's agreements with countries, especially Latin American countries, tend to look like "carbon copies" of Fund agreements.'

Chapter 2, page 41, footnote – 'the Bank has also claimed devaluation in India as its one clear success in exercising leverage.'

Chapter 3, page 5 – 'the World Bank ... "told" New York banks to stop lending in Colombia.'

Chapter 3, page 21 – 'it was felt, rightly or wrongly [by the IMF and World Bank in Chile], that land reform was undesirable, and it was therefore discouraged.'

Chapter 4, page 6 – 'With few exceptions, stabilisation programs supported by the international agencies have resulted in low or zero rates of growth ... during the period when stabilisation was attempted.'

Chapter 4, page 9, footnote – 'the World Bank (in Argentina) was putting pressure on the military government to reduce employment in the railways by 70,000 people, with no views on alternative employment from them, except that they "could always go back to rural areas".'

4. If these were simply the effusions of a journalist with no special access to the Bank, we could hardly object to their publication. But coming from a reputable institution like the ODI, which has a special relationship with the Bank (much exploited in this case), they are quite another matter, and I consider that we have a clear right to insist that publication does not go forward. If there is any question about this, please let me know, because I would want to take the matter up with higher authority. . .

The second memorandum was from the IMF to the IBRD, and was as follows:

. . . I have not had an opportunity to read [the] revised version [of the draft]. One of my colleagues, however, perused it in my absence. It is his conclusion that the paper has not been improved, and very little has been changed in the chapters dealing specifically with the 'nefarious' operations of the international agencies. Accordingly, we still believe that publication of this study would be most undesirable from the Fund and Bank's point of view, although it may be argued that it would do more harm to the ODI than the international agencies. Moreover, we feel, as we did in the first round, that the paper is so tendentious and distorted throughout that it does not lend itself to amendment by specific comments. We intend so to inform Miss Hayter again, though more succinctly and probably more firmly than on the previous occasion. For your information I enclose a copy of my earlier letter to Miss Hayter.

You will recall that [a Bank official] had informed me that, on a visit to London last November, he had taken this matter up with the present head of ODI and had been assured that the paper would not be published. In her covering letter to me, however, Miss Hayter says that 'ODI is now planning to proceed rapidly with publication' ...

Disappointingly, I never did receive a succinct and firm letter from the IMF. However I was given a copy of a letter to the Director of Studies of the ODI from the Chairman of the Development Assistance Committee of the OECD (Organisation for Economic Co-operation and Development), Mr Edwin M. Martin, who was described to me as eminent and progressive; the following are extracts from his letter:

Putting it very broadly, the manuscript reminds me of a comment made in a book by an American humorist after a first visit to England in the Thirties to the effect that English women's shoes of that period looked like they had been made by a cobbler who had had a woman's foot described to him but had never actually seen one. . . . I was surprised to see the table . . . with its naive assumptions, currently popular in some Latin American circles, that the economic impact of foreign investment could be judged from net capital inflows and outflows of interest and dividends on current account.... My recollection is that about 40% of current Latin American export earnings are produced by foreign-owned enterprises ...[5]

Much of his letter was about Cuba and about 'the brutal and repressive police state system which Castro has erected', thus showing quite remarkable weaknesses in his own shoe-making capacities. Finally, he still hoped

that more and more donors, while not prepared to see their money thrown away or used to finance Cuba-type revolutions, will become prepared to put in their own programmes and those of multilateral agencies greater emphasis on development criteria and on the conscious promotion of political and economic change, on which the US is overt leader so far, not excluding the USSR.

In response to ODI's request that the Bank should specify which parts of my study constituted a breach of confidence, the Bank wrote a letter to the Director of ODI which I failed to see. But I was told it had three paragraphs: the first contained the usual complaint that the study was unscholarly, tendentious and inaccurate; the second repeated that the study made use of confidential material supplied by the Bank, which ought not to be revealed; the third stated that the Bank was strongly opposed to publication of the study, and that if the ODI published it, or allowed it to be published elsewhere, this would be a breach of confidence, and the Bank would have to 'draw its own conclusions'. ODI took this to mean that the Bank would withdraw its financial support. This was running, I think, at

5. For a devastating refutation of arguments of this variety, taking them on their own premises, see Laurence Whitehead, 'Aid to Latin America', paper presented to a conference on the Pearson Reports, held at Williamsburg in February 1970, to be published in a volume of conference proceedings by Columbia University Press.

the rate of £6,500 a year, and the total loss was likely to be around £15,000.

ODI was proposing to ask for confirmation that this was a decision on which the highest authorities in the Bank, including McNamara, had been consulted. The Director of ODI had also decided that the decision whether or not to publish must, as a result of the financial implications of publication, be referred to the Executive Committee of the Council of ODI. This was contrary to the assurances I had received, before redrafting the study, that the decision to publish was a matter for the Director alone. It meant that the decision was virtually certain to be negative, since the contents of the study conflicted sharply with the interests of most of the members of the Executive Committee, quite apart from the question of the Bank's financial threats.

I was told that the ODI wanted to assure itself further that the study was in itself worth publishing; and yet more outside advice was sought. I wrote a memorandum to the Director, designed to reassure, saying that before I went to Latin America I had no thesis to which I might have bent the facts, as the Director of the Bank's Western Hemisphere Department maintained, and pointing out that only a few of the bits of information to which Alter objected had actually 'been given to me in confidence' by the Bank or the Fund; some others had been obtained elsewhere and had subsequently been confirmed by Bank officials. Bank officials knew what I was doing, and knew they didn't like it, so

they revealed what they wanted to reveal. Alter himself was particularly cagey, and most of the interview [with him] was occupied by his trying to find out what my conclusions on leverage were likely to be, and impressing on me the secret nature of the whole operation (hence the quotation to which he objects). In general, Bank co-operation was not as full and free as they are claiming.... Most of the points to which Alter objects are quite important evidence for what I have to say, which is perhaps the main reason why he objects to them.... I have thought carefully whether the points are accurate. They are all based on sources and evidence which I believe to be reliable, and I am certain that I have reported them accurately. If Bank officials have made inaccurate statements, or believe that others have, they should possibly be given yet another opportunity to correct them; but I think, from my conversation with [a Bank official], that it is unlikely that they will help on this, that the problem, as far as the Bank is concerned, is not the accuracy of the study but the nature of the views expressed, and that publication, if it is decided upon, should not be held up in the hope of receiving further useful comments from the Bank. I personally feel confident that what I have said is as accurate as possible, and certainly does not distort the evidence.

The Director of the ODI responded to one of the points in my memorandum, as follows: '... to reassure you about your last paragraph ..., the point I made to [the Bank] a year ago was that the study would not be published in its then form ...'

The next instalment in this small saga came in a series of communications from a member of the ODI staff, proposing that he should redraft parts of the study. He suggested that if he did so the Council might well agree to publication, and that 'the Bank's attitude' actually increased rather than diminished the chances of publication. But ODI would have to feel convinced about the value of the study. 'ODI, after all, is not an academic institute. It is aimed at policy, and it is in those terms that we shall have to defend the decision to publish ...' The issue of 'leverage' needed to be publicly discussed:

... We are all a bit bothered, though, when it comes to the ideological framework in which the empirical study is set....

You may reasonably reply that your specific conclusions are indissolubly a part of the wider ideological framework ... but in that case I think the counter-argument might be that it is not ODI's function to publish ideological dissertations, of the right, left *or* centre.... The other two questions – concerning points of fact and points of confidentiality – are more or less settled. It seems to be accepted now that perfect corroboration is not possible in a study of this kind and that the Bank has been given every opportunity to make its points: on confidentiality, the point made in your latest comments also seems to be accepted.

If I wanted to retain 'the ideological character', then I would have to find another publisher. But then the conclusions 'would lose the impact on policy-makers[6] that they would have under an ODI label ...' So he had suggested a way of 'protecting the ODI from vulnerability...' A 'small group' would

go right through the draft and pare it down to the hard-hitting essentials, also incorporating, in order to strengthen its persuasive power on officials, the standard journalistic glosses – 'usually reliable sources' etc. No changes of fact *or interpretation* would be involved so far as Parts [chapters] 1–3 are concerned. On Part 4, we might have to be more savage. The whole of Cuba would have to go ... and most of the revolutionary prescription.

I wrote back saying, among other things:

You're falling into the World Bank's error: saying that ODI books are not 'ideological' when in fact they are (you *know* they are), but their ideology is not usually made explicit – although I could give a lot of quotations from ODI publications, including mine, whose ideological content is pretty clear ... (shall I?). What's mainly wrong with my latest effort is not that it has an ideological framework, but that it's the *wrong one* – and perhaps also that it's made more explicit than usual.

6. This represented one of the differences between us: I had no expectations from the 'policy-makers'.

I also suggested that it would be an extremely difficult task to disentangle 'leverage' from politics.

I wrote a conciliatory letter to the Director of the ODI, asking for clarification before I decided about re-drafting:

... For example I wondered whether you had had further confirmation from the Bank that they would discontinue their financial support if ODI published the study ...? ... Perhaps [the] re-drafting is more likely to affect Ex Co [the Executive Committee]'s decision than the Bank's, but supposing the Bank withdrew its threat in any case, presumably you wouldn't have to refer the issue of publication to Ex Co?

I also asked for confirmation that I could publish elsewhere, especially as the Bank had said they would cut off their support if ODI 'allowed' the study to be published. Did the ODI have a legal, as well as a moral, right to stop me from publishing (which, for example, the Bank could penalize the ODI for not using)?

In reply, the Director wrote in the following terms:

... As regards the issues involved, we have heard nothing more from the Bank, although I may learn more from Lars Lind, when he passes through London on October 2. While the question of publication must now be an Ex Co decision, because of the issues that have been raised, I hope that the action that the Bank may or may not take will not be the central issue. What we want to be sure of is: given that we may have a battle with the Bank on this, are we sure in our own minds about the quality of the study, and the importance of its findings? On both, I think the answer is 'yes' on the central issue of leverage, qualified by doubts about the broader conclusions which do not seem to follow so clearly from your evidence. As I think ... has [been] explained to you, it is Ex Co that we have to convince now, not the Bank.

As regards the question of your publishing the study elsewhere, I cannot see that we have any right, legally or otherwise, to stop you doing so. If we had such a right, we would be in an awkward position, since as you know the Bank has expressed the strong view that the study should not be published, by ODI or by anyone else. Should ODI not publish the study, you would therefore be entitled to publish it elsewhere, if you wished – in the full knowledge of the Bank's view ...

I also received a second long letter on the question of re-drafting, saying:

... Of course you are right in saying that all studies have an ideological content, and that the W[orld]B[ank]'s objection to yours is that it's the wrong one. But ... from ODI's point of view, in particular, the question is not whether you have chosen the 'right' ideology, but what place it occupies in your total framework ...

My study could have demonstrated that 'within the frame-work of the established ideology', certain results followed from the policy of leverage, and it could perhaps have stated that these results were unsatisfactory. Instead, it attempted to show '... that the established ideology produces certain self-evidently undesirable results, the contrary of which can only be achieved by the application of an alternative (stated) ideology...' This was inadmissible, since it would require '*much* more empirical work' for its substantiation. Therefore my conclusions on leverage could be retained, but the 'alternative prescription' must be left out, since otherwise the argument would be circular, confusing conclusions with evidence. All very complicated, as the proposed editor admitted. In addition, he wanted me to attribute my evidence to its sources in a less provocative manner, '... without giving an *a priori* impression that you are some kind of cunning spy ...'; for example I should not refer specifically to Policy Memorandum 204, and to the fact that it is not published.

I wrote back, wondering why the 'logical defects' had 'suddenly taken on so much importance', and saying:

... The conclusion I've reached is that, given the very great differences in our points of view, I don't believe you would be able to change the draft in such a way that it would satisfy us both.... You see I absolutely don't accept the limitations – 'within the framework of the established ideology' – you impose in ... your 'acceptable' subjects for research ... [The study] merely points out that 'the application of an alternative ideology' *may* be the only solution, and that such a solution would be unacceptable to the international agencies.... I don't have to prove that the alternative *is* the only solution and I don't try to – nor do I recommend the solution.

I said I had made some small changes to make this clearer, and had cut out one or two 'naïve political effusions' of an 'inaccurately pinkish variety'. But I didn't agree that the section on Cuba should go: 'the fact that there appears to be such a taboo on Cuba does rather prove my case.' I also thought that:

Your proposal on Policy Memorandum 204 merely introduces a tone of approval and understanding of the World Bank, unnecessarily in this case I should have thought. I actually think it's quite seriously scandalous that Policy Memo. 204 should be a *secret*, quite apart from its existence. And I don't think that the Bank's internal memoranda are 'very easy to obtain' – d'you really think they'd give me a copy of 204 if I asked, any more than they showed me the other internal documents I asked ... to see? And one has to know that they exist ...

I said that if ODI decided against publication of the draft as it stood, I would try to publish it elsewhere.

I also wrote to the Director, saying I did not want to have the study cut,

because I really believe that a study of leverage which did not mention and deal with the wider political issues would be inadequate and misleading.... I think that much of the discussion of leverage, performance criteria and so on ... is unrealistic, rather pointless ... because no attempt is made to recognise, and evaluate the importance of, the general political constraints in the aid-giving process.

I am in addition very much opposed to any further 'watering down' of the study ...

After the 7 October meeting of the Executive Committee of the ODI, I received the following letter from the Director:

As promised, I am writing to let you know the outcome of the meeting this week of the Executive Committee of ODI Council, when the question of publishing your study on leverage was fully discussed. I am very sorry to have to tell you that the decision was against publication.

I am afraid this will be a great disappointment to you, and, indeed, the Committee reached its decision with considerable reluctance. Your draft had been read by various members of Council, including four of those present at the meeting, and its potential quality and importance was not in dispute. But unfortunately the combined views of specialist referees showed that it still contained weaknesses in construction, balance and accuracy, and in the light of these criticisms the Committee could not endorse its publication.

The Committee was of course aware of the views of the World Bank, and of its opposition to publication. But I can assure you that this influenced the decision only to the extent that it was felt that in such circumstances ODI had to be completely confident about the craftsmanship of any study that was published – since it would obscure subsequent debate if fundamental hostility to the conclusions of the study could be presented as valid criticisms of its technical competence. This confidence was, I am afraid, lacking; and since you were not prepared to allow further editing of the present draft to be undertaken inside ODI, there was unanimous agreement not to proceed further.

This is a very disappointing outcome, not only for you but also for all of us in ODI who have tried to bring to completion a study suitable for publication. I can only assure you that it was arrived at with reluctance, and after thorough consideration that was in no sense lacking in sympathy.

I wrote back, once more, saying that I was looking for another publisher, again asking to see a copy of the Bank's threatening letter, and claiming that

your suggestion that the grounds for deciding against publication were mainly technical does conflict rather with earlier ODI comments, with the comments of outsiders, and with the nature of [the] proposals for editing the study. I should find it quite understandable if ODI decided against publication *either* because, as [the letters quoted above] made plain, the conclusions of the study conflicted too sharply with ODI policies; *or* because ODI was not prepared to risk losing the Bank's money; but I should like to be told the real reasons for rejection, and to have some idea of the nature of the discussion which took place in Ex Co.

I got the following reply:

Thank you for your letter of October 13th.

I do not think that I can usefully add anything to my letter of October 9th, which explained why the Executive Committee decided against publication of your study by ODI.

As regards the letter from the World Bank, you will remember I told you, when I indicated its gist, that it was addressed to me in confidence and I was respecting that confidence.

That was my final communication with the ODI.

GLOSSARY

Bretton Woods	Place at which the founding conference of the IMF and the World Bank took place, in 1946.
Compensatory finance	Money provided to compensate for shortfalls in export earnings below an expected level; name given to an IMF scheme doing this.
Cost-push inflation	Inflation which is caused by autonomous increases in prices, such as higher charges for electricity or other industrial inputs, rather than by increases in demand or supply bottlenecks.
Counterpart funds	Local currency acquired from the sale of foreign exchange provided as aid.
International liquidity	The amount of convertible money available for the financing of international trade, mainly gold, dollars and sterling.
Liberalization of imports	The removal or reduction of restrictions on imports such as tariffs and quotas.
Monetarist	Description of policies designed to cure inflation mainly through 'orthodox' methods such as controlling the supply of money.
Multilateralization of aid	The provision of aid through an international institution to which national 'donors' contribute, rather than giving their money directly, or 'bilaterally', to the underdeveloped country which receives it.
Shortfall	Expression used to describe the amount by which exports are below their expected level.
Stand-by agreement	Agreement which governments make with the IMF enabling them to draw money from the IMF up to an agreed amount during the period covered by the agreement when and if they need it.
Structuralist	Description of policies, designed to cure inflation, which do not rely on orthodox 'monetar-

ist' methods but demand a more fundamental restructuring of the economy, on the grounds that inflation is caused mainly by bottlenecks in supply, which cannot be removed without an effort to reorganize and expand production.

Supplementary
finance

Another way of saying compensatory finance; name used by the World Bank.

INDEX